Race Across Canada

Peter Keen

Published by Peter Keen
Publishing Partner: Paragon Publishing, Rothersthorpe
First published 2024

© Peter Keen 2024

The rights of Peter Keen to be identified as the author of this work have been asserted by him in accordance with the Copyright, Designs and Patents Act of 1988.

All rights reserved; no part of this publication may be reproduced, stored in a retrieval system, or transmitted in any form or by any means, electronic, mechanical, photocopying, recording or otherwise without the prior written consent of the publisher or a licence permitting copying in the UK issued by the Copyright Licensing Agency Ltd. www.cla.co.uk

ISBN 978-1-78792-063-7

Book design, layout and production management by Into Print
www.intoprint.net
+44 (0)1604 832149

Contents

- Acknowledgements ... 4
- Introduction ... 5
- Arranging Flights and Car Hire ... 7
- Essential Paperwork ... 8
- Buying things in Canada ... 10
- Driving in Canada ... 12
- Eating Out ... 15
- Phrases ... 16
- Getting There ... 17
- Toronto to Niagara Falls ... 22
- Niagara Falls to Sault Ste Marie ... 26
- Sault Ste Marie to Thunder Bay ... 30
- Thunder Bay to Steinbach ... 35
- Steinbach to Regina ... 42
- Regina to Medicine Hat ... 46
- Medicine Hat to Calgary ... 50
- Calgary to Banff ... 54
- Banff to Rocky Mountain House ... 59
- At Rocky Mountain House ... 64
- Rocky Mountain House to Hinton ... 67
- Hinton to McBride ... 72
- McBride to Blue River and back to McBride ... 75
- Mc Bride to Houston ... 79
- Houston to Prince Rupert ... 83
- At Prince Rupert ... 87
- At Prince Rupert ... 92
- Prince Rupert to Port Hardy ... 94
- At Port Hardy ... 96
- Port Hardy to Campbell River ... 99
- Campbell River to Tofino and return ... 103
- Campbell River to Cobble Hill ... 108
- Cobble Hill, Chemainus, and Victoria ... 110
- Cobble Hill to Whistler ... 115
- Whistler to Clinton ... 119
- Clinton to Blue River ... 123
- Blue River to Mount Robson and return ... 127
- Blue River to Banff ... 132
- Banff to Creston ... 136
- Creston to Grand Forks ... 140
- Grand Forks to Princeton ... 145
- Princeton to Hope ... 151
- Hope area ... 156
- Hope to Vancouver ... 158
- Vancouver ... 162
- Homeward bound ... 164
- Conclusion ... 167

Acknowledgements

My grateful thanks go to Nick and Heather Rees for proof reading this account, and for their helpful suggestions in presentation.

My gratitude also goes to Into Print for design, layout, and production.

I thank my neighbours and friends Nick, Heather, Clint, and Darcie for getting my trip under way after the failure of the public transport network. Also, for friends Andy and Ali for my safe return home at journey's end.

Thanks go to friends Don and Kim who accommodated me at their home in Vancouver Island, and for their guided tour of Victoria, and of highlights of the south of the island, and for their kindness and hospitality.

My thanks to Bob and Joan, who are now my friends from Missouri, and who provided company and lovely conversation during time in Prince Rupert, and on the long ferry crossing to Vancouver Island.

My thanks go to Sara of Penybont Inn, for feeding my fish while I was away.

My thanks go to many people across Canada who took an interest in my trip, and provided much information along the route.

Introduction

I had since childhood wanted to visit Canada. I still have my first world atlas that has been a treasured book for over sixty years. It offers three centres of access to the world by air. They are London, Winnipeg, and Sydney. The name Winnipeg fascinated me, with its position central to the second largest country on earth. I learned about the huge Rocky Mountain range at school, and had always wanted to see it.

Older age has brought the opportunity to explore places of interest, and now, Canada has brought a great set of experiences that I would like to share with you.

Any trip of this magnitude demands a degree of preparation, and there are expenses that need to be considered. The basic preparation is simple. How will you get to Canada? What time of year will you go? Where will you travel when you are there? How will you travel? What funds are needed? Where will you stay? What documents are required?

I decided to travel across Canada from East to West. The reasoning behind this direction is that if you set off each day travelling west, you have the sun behind you. If you go from West to East, the sun is in your eyes, especially early in the day. I was interested in travel by train and researched the Rocky Mountaineer as the transport of choice through the mountains. The big issue with train travel is that the train stops at scheduled stations. You have no independence. With private transport, you have total independence to travel where you wish at the time you wish. I decided to hire a self-drive car and travel from Toronto to Vancouver as the basic spine of the trip, but to include other areas as time permitted.

I negotiated a five-and-a-half-week period off work with my employer, and asked Liberty Travel of Oswestry to come up with options for flights to and from Canada, and car hire. The best option for the flights appeared to be Air Canada at a return cost of £1265.00. The most competitive car hire was with Hertz at a total cost of £3485. There was a hefty one-way charge with the car, of £800. The idea is that someone from the company has to bring your car back from Vancouver to Toronto. The truth is that I travelled East to West, but others would travel the other way, and could drive the car back. A company as large as Hertz has the capacity to work one way travel in that manner, but they choose to impose a one-way surcharge.

I arranged travel insurance through the Post Office to cover any medical and other problems, and the cost was £318. This depends on age and existing medical history.

I ordered three sheet maps, one of the whole of Canada, one of East Canada, and one of West Canada. Sheet maps are a good way of assessing overall progress and where to go. Sheet maps are useless when you are driving, but would be great if you had a companion to do the navigation and tell you where to go. For me, it's great to spread them on the bed when I get to my night's accommodation, and consider the next move. I have a TomTom satellite navigator which I have used for many trips to Australia and New Zealand, and it's just great. It's well short of perfection, but is extremely useful, and I'd go as far as to say that for a lone driver, it would be hard to manage without it. I downloaded the most recent Canada mapping to it just before I set off. It's simple to use. You enter the place you wish to drive to, and it calculates routes. You select the route and at each step, it tells you what to do.

I left packing till the last minute. I always travel light with one small case, and a little bag in which my tablets and paperwork go. The airports are full of people pushing trolleys full of massive suitcases and various other belongings. At the beginning of the nineteenth century, Jerome K Jerome wrote two books about three men holidaying. They learned to take things they couldn't manage without, rather than all the things they thought they could do with. It's a strategy that people should get to learn today. On holiday, all you need is a few clothes, your camera, tablets, shaver, TomTom, maps, paperwork, and very little else. There is absolutely no need and no point in taking all the stuff people pack. And, here's another thing. They want to bring lots on board the plane in bags too large for the overhead lockers. These then have to go in sideways and make space problems for other more thoughtful travellers. There are little wire cages at check-in. Your bag should fit in the cage. Many cases that people take on board won't, and check-in staff should make people check those bags in. I researched the right size for the wire cage, and I stick to it. This makes life easy for me and for others. At my destination, I don't have to wait for cases to appear on carousels. I've had cases that have been damaged and even lost by baggage handlers. I've had all these problems when I used to take a case big enough to climb in. Not anymore.

I booked a night in a place just outside Heathrow for the night before my flight. It's always best to do this rather than trying to get to London on the day of departure. Public transport is far too unreliable for that sort of thing.

I made all necessary arrangements about six months before departure, with the exception of train tickets. You can only book them a few weeks in advance.

Once all the arrangements have been made, I try to dismiss them from my mind and press on with the activities for each day. You frequently hear the expression "I can't wait", with regard to a desired activity. While you look forward to things, they are gone in a flash, so it's best to make what you can from each day as it comes along.

I have arranged this book in the form of a daily log with each day headed with the date and kilometre reading on the hire car, together with fuel purchases in litres and Canadian dollars. This enables you to see the distance covered and the daily itinerary.

Some of the opinions I present in this book may be different to yours. That's fine. Thankfully, we are allowed to hold views and mention them. Hopefully, our views are reasoned out, and we can discuss them, and arrive at a mutual understanding.

Arranging Flights and Car Hire

I asked Liberty Travel of Oswestry to do this for me. I supplied the dates from 24th July to 30th August 2023, and they did the rest.

It turned out that Air Canada had the best deal on flights at £1265 return. I could have arranged flights with stops, but I dislike flying intensely, and much prefer to get it over with in one go each way. I wanted to fly to Toronto in one hop and fly back from Vancouver in one hop. This is possible, provided you use London Heathrow as your UK airport. A direct flight from Manchester to Toronto is possible, but not back from Vancouver. I accepted the findings of Liberty Travel and paid the bill.

Car hire is a muddle. Hiring for a few weeks is much more expensive than for a few days. Many companies do not offer unlimited mileage, which means that if you do a high mileage, you end up with a massive bill when you return the car. You have to pay a one-way surcharge if your drop off point is different to the pick-up point. Many hirers operate away from the airports and on arrival you have to call the hirer to take you to and from the airport. This isn't a big issue, but you have to factor the time involved into your plans. Many hirers expect you to have insurance. There will be an excess to pay in the event of theft, fire, or other damage to the car. The excess varies considerably. If you wish to avoid the excess, you can pay an additional premium, and this will usually be hundreds of pounds over a few weeks of hire. There will usually be exclusions expressed in the small print of your hire. You need to ensure that those exclusions do not impact on your travel plans. You can be sure, as noted in Parkinson's Law of Universal Cussedness, that any problems with your car will occur while you are travelling in an exclusion zone, if there is one.

I accepted Hertz with pick-up and drop-off within the airport, and with unlimited mileage, and with a £500 excess.

Essential Paperwork

You need your Passport with at least six months to run at the time of your arrival in Canada. There's always the possibility that you might have to stay in Canada should something go wrong. Your passport is scrutinised at check-in, and if you don't have six months validity, the chances are that your dream trip will come to an abrupt end, and you will be on the next available train home.

You apparently need a visa to visit Canada. Liberty Travel arranged this for me. I believe the cost is £7. They don't call it a visa now. It's called an "eTA". In my profession, "A" normally stands for "arrival". For example, "ETA" means "Expected Time of Arrival". "DNA" means "Did not Arrive". "DOA" means "Dead on Arrival". However, in travel plans, "eTA" means "Electronic Travel Authorisation". For travel to Canada, the time of expiry is March 2026, so travel permission is very generous. It is an easy process to arrange the eTA, but I asked Liberty Travel if they would kindly do this for me. I'm told it's an essential arrangement. I had a hardcopy of my eTA and I proudly furnished this on arrival in Canada. The officials simply weren't interested in looking at it. They said, "you keep that". Whether or not I would have been admitted without it, I don't know. What I do know is that for Canada, the price is small, and it's easy to arrange, so it isn't worth the risk of turning up in Canada without it.

You don't need travel and medical insurance, and I have travelled to many parts of the world without it. If something goes wrong, you'll probably regret not having it. I always used OK 2 Travel, and found them cheap and good at coping with clients who have existing medical conditions, provided they are treated and stable. However, there was a problem a few years ago and I had to speak to an operative on the telephone. That was when the arrangement unravelled, because they will not provide insurance if there is any unpaid voluntary work during your travel, as is the case on my Cambodia trips. I now use the Post Office. I have made the arrangement at the Post Office counter, which was nice. They don't allow that anymore. You have to do it online. They cope with existing medical conditions, but the price escalates for each thing you have wrong with you. If you breeze through life on no more than an occasional paracetamol, your travel insurance will be cheap. If you are a walking medical encyclopaedia, it may be the most expensive part of the travel. Mine is sort of medium, at £318 for the five-week trip.

You don't need a Covid Pass to travel to Canada at this moment in time. That may alter, as folk keep announcing different variants of the virus, and worrying folk with the thing. The point is that you can offer your arms as pin cushions for those making a lot of money from Covid vaccines. It probably won't stop you getting Covid, or passing it on. Sorry, if this statement is controversial, but I believe it to be proven fact. Vaccines may reduce the severity of the disease, and may reduce your viral load. However, the whole vaccine program is money driven, and by money, I'm talking about the main producers making $1000 per second out of the vaccines. It's a fact that any company netting that sort of profit, will be reluctant to jack it in, regardless of the benefits. Covid is a coronavirus, closely related to the common cold. We can die from a cold and we can die from

Covid. However, the natural resistance grows each time we get these things, which is why colds get less frequent as we get older, provided we eat and exercise healthily. I believed from the outset, that Covid was a panic driver initially, led by those who should have known better, and, as we are exposed to the virus over time, it will become no more dramatic than the cold. The cold is such an overrated sickness that people will not tell you they have one. Instead, they tell you they have a nasty dose of flu. It's the only way of securing sympathy for feeling miserable for a week. Anyway, we digress. You don't need evidence of vaccination at present.

I did not book accommodation for my trip around Canada. I winged it on the way. However, I did book my first night's stay at Niagara Falls. The reason for this is that when you go through security on arrival, many countries ask where you will be staying. You can tell them that you have no fixed abode and will be travelling round. I've found that story difficult to get past them. It seems unusual to their trained ears. I've only got a total of 10lbs of luggage and there is clearly no tent in my possession, and the officials start to probe deeper. It's nice and easy if you can give them a name and address of your first night's stay. I always fix this and have a hardcopy of the reservation in my bag. You can then furnish this if the official asks you. If they don't ask, don't mention it. There is no point prolonging these interviews. Just tell them what they think they need to know, is my advice.

You don't really need airline tickets, but I always take them. The airline will know who is travelling on each flight, and all they want to see is your passport. However, if there is a mix-up of some kind, your tickets and proof of payment may go a long way to resolving the issue. I have observed issues of this nature getting quite serious with people going off into private rooms to continue the dispute. For a couple of A4 sheets, it's comforting to have the documents with you, but in years of travelling, I've never been asked to produce them. I did have a problem once when I was in Cambodia. I travelled from there on a one-way ticket to Thailand. It worked fine, but on the way back to Cambodia, I had an awful job with the official. She couldn't accept a one-way ticket. In the end I told this lady that I had purchased the ticket, and wanted to travel one-way, and her job was to enable my flight. I said that if she wasn't happy, I was happy for her to fetch the manager. At that point she stopped being difficult. The other thing is that unnecessary bother of this nature tends to reduce as the check-in area gets busy. If they spend a lot of time with everyone, the plane doesn't get off the ground. If you turn up really early as I do, they can afford the time to be as picky as they like.

Take your car hire voucher with you, and check what additional money they will want off you when you arrive. You will have already paid for the car hire, and that has earned them interest from the day you paid it. You will still need to pay a few hundred pounds deposit. And your one-way surcharge, and any additional insurance you want, when you arrive to pick the car up.

Buying things in Canada

In the UK, we are used to seeing the prices of goods fixed to the products, and usually to the shelf they are on as well. That price is what you pay. This is not the case in Canada, including supermarkets. Taxes of various kinds are added to your items when you pay. If you aren't expecting this, it can be a bit of a shock. Many shop keepers would rather the display price be what you pay, but that's not the way they do it.

Tips are generally paid, even for a drink, and 15% is the minimum you are expected to donate. They prefer 20% or 25%. That would add so much to the price, that they have to get by on 15% from old codgers like me. You can elect to refuse to pay a gratuity, and on occasion when service or product did not meet expectation, I did so, but it is considered bad form. I've not found anywhere in the world where such a high level of tipping is expected, but I understand that it's the same in the USA. It seems that is a continental issue with the whole of North America involved.

The same issue is experienced when you use Booking.com to secure and pay for accommodation. In many countries, the price displayed on the Booking.com page, is what you pay. This is not the case in Canada. You will pay additional taxes and other costs like cleaning. You would expect the room rental to include toiletries and cleaning. In Canada, the room and the furnishings are usually included, but other costs are extra. Some places double the cost with these additions, and you have to be very careful to read the small print before accepting and paying. Booking.com gives the option of paying immediately, or paying when you arrive. I paid before arrival if that option was available. That avoids the problem caused when places try to make you pay more than the agreed price when you get there. I did have that a couple of times, and it's embarrassing to have to show them the agreed price on your phone. Many accommodations include free parking, but again, it's wise to check the small print. Because some charge extra for parking, and it can be quite a lot.

You also need to be aware that if you hire a car in Canada, there are several fees to pay. There is the car obviously, but there are taxes, and a very high one-way surcharge if you are dropping off at a different place to where you are picking it up. Ensure that you have unlimited mileage included. Some allow you a fixed distance, and then a per kilometre charge after that. You will also pay a deposit, which they aren't good at refunding when you return the car in good condition. They never pay it back when you return the car. They say it comes back after a period of time. There is also insurance to pay. You can pay the basic fire and theft insurance, but if anything happens, you can end up paying for the car. You are advised to arrange your own insurance cover, or accept the more expensive insurance offered by the car hire company. Even after paying that, there will be an excess, which is usually $500 or more. This means that you will pay the excess no matter what mishap occurs. For a booking of a few weeks, something is almost bound to go wrong. I only had a smashed windscreen, and a puncture, and I paid for them both myself. It's no good saying that the mishap wasn't your fault. Although you are probably not to blame, the car hire company takes the view that it happened while the vehicle was in your care and therefore, it's your problem. There is no compassion, mitigation, or half way meeting point with these problems. You are just saddled with them. However, private car hire gives you the flexibility to travel when and where you want, and that independence is a wonderful thing.

Driving in Canada

You would expect that whatever country you are in, that driving would be similar. Well, you'd be wrong.

For a start you drive on the right instead of the left. That comes intuitively in Canada when you hire a car there because it has a left-hand drive. You will find yourself getting into the wrong side of the car sometimes, and this is embarrassing when folk are watching, but once you are in the driving seat with a steering wheel in front of you, it comes naturally.

Road rules are very different to the UK. We are used to red traffic lights meaning stop until they turn green. Once they've turned green, you then wait another period of time while the UK drivers notice that the colour change has occurred, and another period while they prepare their vehicle for forward motion, and another period of time while they actually get it moving. In Canada, a red traffic light only means stop if you are turning left, or going straight on. If you are turning right, you are meant to go if it's safe to do so. If you don't go while indicating right, you will hear horns blowing a lot. They mean, why aren't you going, you noodle. Some right turns at red traffic lights aren't permitted. There will be extra signage to tell you when that's the case. It's all a bit confusing.

Another thing you'll find is that at cross roads, particularly in towns, there is a system of who arrives first has the right of way. You have to stop, even when you can see that it's clear to go. The rolling stop is illegal, and if the police spot you not completely stopping, they will do you. All this is foreign to the UK where you always have a main and minor road. Those on the minor road are meant to stop until it's safe to go. Many don't. They just pull out in front of you and then dither for miles. But in Canada, at the crossroads everybody stops, and priority goes to whoever arrived first. If two arrive at precisely the same time, priority goes to the guy on the right.

Driving psyche of different nations is very different to the UK. In the UK, a large percentage of drivers travel at half to two thirds of the road speed. That doesn't happen in Canada. They all travel at least at the road speed limit, and normally quite a bit more. You won't get liked for holding a great queue up at slow speed, like people do in the UK. While delaying tactics and queue making is considered ok in the UK, it certainly isn't in Canada. You will get a lot of adverse signage and noise if you try it. So, if you are one of the people that likes to drive like a twig in a brook at marginally over the speed of continental drift, you need a change of tactic when you try driving in Canada. You need to keep up with the traffic flow. It's far safer to do so rather than cause obstruction and frustration.

You'll find a lot of places in Canada where you'd like to stop and take a photograph. Well usually, you can't, because they don't have laybys at those places. This is frustrating. There may be a layby further back or forwards, but not at the viewpoint. If there is a layby on the opposite side of the road, you are often not allowed to use it. There is frequently a sign before the layby saying no left turn. The idea is to stop you crossing the opposing traffic flow, and to avoid you holding up your lane while waiting for it to be safe to cross. Most roads in Canada are very busy. You would expect a country with half our population and over 40 times our size to be quiet, but it isn't. The only quiet roads are ones that don't go anywhere, or the grit ones. Once you are on a main road, you are in a fast-moving stream of traffic.

Another sign you will see a lot of is one with a big black splodge in the middle. That means you can't stop here. They use these to indicate an avalanche or rock fall area, or anywhere else where they don't want you stopping, even when it looks like a layby. If you leave your car there, it won't still be there when you get back. It will have been towed away, and you won't have a clue where to find it, and you may have a very long walk, and a big bill.

When you want to fill up with fuel, in eastern Canada, it's like the UK. You fill up and pay in the kiosk. When you move further west, you have to pay at the pump or in the kiosk before you fill up. The default amount taken from your card is usually $200, and they refund the amount you haven't used. There is the option to have a smaller amount than $200, and I got the feel for how much I needed to fill up. You don't want the technology sucking $200 off you for $20 worth of fuel, so set it a little more than what you need. In western Canada, they obviously don't trust you to pay for the fuel you've dispensed into your tank. In the UK, they trust you to wander across to the kiosk and pay afterwards. If you decide not to pay, you need to be aware that a lot of very good quality photographs of your theft are immediately sent through to the police and they will be after you within a short distance.

Another thing you'll notice is that Canadians hardly ever reverse into a parking place. They want you to know that they've arrived so they scorch into their place head first, and get out and lock the door. Door locking is designed to sound the horn, so that everyone turns round to notice your arrival. In the UK, we reverse into our place. If you work for the police or other organisation that teaches advanced driving, you will be taught to reverse in as a matter of course. The reason is eminently sensible. If you head in forwards, you have to reverse out into the traffic flow, with poor visibility on either side due to other vehicles parked by you. It's far safer to head out forwards into the traffic flow. Canadians tend to leave their engines running for long periods while stationary. If they've backed up to a motel room, they fill it with fumes, so that is the one and only place where forward parking is necessary. I don't leave my engine running when I stop. It's a waste of fuel. People think they have to do it to let the turbo cool down. It just isn't needed these days. Park and switch off.

Speed limits in Canada are very varied, and repeat signs are not as frequent as in the UK. The general view is that the police won't bother them unless they are doing more than 20kph above the speed limit, so that's what they do. The fact is that any excess is an offence. A lot of roads have signs telling you what the penalty is for each leap above the limit that you drive at. The first fining point is 20kph above the limit, when you'll be charged about $95. The fine for 30kph above the limit is $220. For 40kph above the limit, you'll pay $295, and above that, you're looking at your licence and your car being taken off you. Impatient drivers, driving at high speeds are a problem, and I saw several pulled over by police in unmarked cars.

Lane discipline tends to be fairly good in the UK. In Canada, the principle is the same, but the practice is different. You aren't meant to cross a solid line in the centre of the road, and especially not when it's a double one. They do though when they want to overtake and think they can get away with it. Another thing with lane discipline is that you are meant to stay in the nearside lane unless you are overtaking. If you don't, they will overtake on the other side, and that is ok in Canada. Be aware of this, and keep in unless you are overtaking something. In the UK, you aren't allowed to overtake on the inside, even though, for people driving slowly in the centre lane of a motorway, it would be a nice option.

The roads are generally wide and well surfaced, and given this quantum leap in quality compared with the UK, you'd expect that safety statistics would be much better. Well, you'd be wrong because the accident rates in Canada are double what they are in the UK. I believe that this is in part due to the ridiculous driving behaviour of some people, and poor road layout in some cases. There are thousands of minor bumps in the UK that don't get reported because some people don't drive fast enough to bend metal when they hit something. But whatever the reason, there is a high serious accident rate in Canada, and you have to try and avoid this by driving with alertness and good sense.

The TomTom or similar device is a wonderful help. You can't safely read a map at the wheel, so a device that tells you what to do is great. Download the most recent mapping to it before you come. You will notice later that many addresses were not well navigated by my TomTom, but for finding towns, it was really good. Many rural routes in Canada are not paved. They are grit roads, or varying quality. They are slow, dusty, or very muddy after rain. They have horizontal ridges milled across them and are very bumpy to drive on sometimes. I set my TomTom to avoid unpaved roads, and it did this well, but sometimes got it wrong. A grit road will add hours to a long journey, but they do offer peaceful motoring, and the opportunity to get off the beaten track.

Roadworks are a national problem in Canada and the UK. However, in Canada, lengthy holdups are frequently encountered. Road closures are not as common as in the UK, but you can wait a long time for your turn through a construction site.

Eating Out

In the UK we are familiar with the concept of healthy eating. We have KFC, MacDonalds, Fish n Chips and other fast-food chains. Some will try and tell you that they are healthy, and if that sort of thing is ok with you, then that's fine. Fried stuff is simply not the best healthy option for every meal. We like meat or fish and two veg to get the right balance of essential nutrients and food value to maintain good health and temper. We are what we eat, and it is very important to get this balance right.

Unless I was looking in the wrong places, I found little options for what I'd call healthy options in Canada. It was nearly all fast-food. In restaurants, you'd see little evidence of vegetables, but lots of folk chewing their way through big steaks. There are lots of opportunities for three fry-ups per day. Much of the time, if you want greens, you have to specifically order a side salad. Greens don't come as a matter of course with a meal.

As for drinks, it's nearly all lager, wine, or coke. There is little real ale on tap. It is coming, and there are a number of micro-breweries. Water is available free. Most tap water is safe in Canada, and when it isn't, they will normally tell you.

Remember that in addition to the prices shown on menus, there will be taxes, and the expected tip of a minimum of 15%. If you pay by card, the tip is usually shown by three buttons on the card machine. You press the 15%, 20%, or 25% button to add the tip onto your bill.

Phrases

A few phrases crop up regularly, and have a different meaning than in the UK. Here are a few examples. You may come across more.

If you go to look at a view, a Canadian will go to check it out. To us, checking out is a diagnostic process to find a fault, as with a car engine making a strange noise. Another example is a policeman who will check out something considered suspicious.

If you are uncertain of the way forward, you will look at the options and "work out" a plan. A Canadian will "figure it out" instead.

Frequently, you will be asked how you are going. It means, how are you? You might not be going anywhere. You may be sitting in a deckchair, but a Canadian will ask you how you are going. They do the same in Australia and New Zealand, and I believe in the USA. It's a method of greeting and enquiring into your welfare.

If options are presented to you in Canada, you would tend to reply by saying, "I'd like that option please". A Canadian would reply by saying, "that option works for me". What "works for me" means, it's ok.

If we like something in the UK, we will say it's good, or wonderful etc. A Canadian will declare "that's arsum", which means awesome. It translates as anything that's on the right side of ok. You get the idea when you are asked to complete a multi-choice survey. Most are presented in the form of five faces. The first is a great big grin. The next one is a smile. The third has a flat line for the mouth which means ok, or average. Then there is a mouth turned down looking grumpy. Finally, there is a face that looks ready to weep. "Arsum" would be either of the two smiley faces.

Getting There

I don't know why, but my travel arrangements are normally saddled with trauma. I've just grown to accept this as one of life's problems. However, on 24th July 2023 at 7am, I made my way in the drizzle to the Penybont bus stop to get the 7:16 bus into Oswestry. It didn't come. I waited until 7:30 and phoned my friend and near neighbour, Nick, and he said he would give me a lift to Gobowen station, where I was to catch the 10:14 service to Birmingham International. The service appeared on the electronic board as "on time". I had plenty of time, so I ordered a vegetarian breakfast and coffee in the Derwen Café within the station building. Part way through breakfast, garbled messages started coming through from different station officials. It turned out that all services in both directions were cancelled due to animals on the line near Chirk. At this time, the electronic board still maintained that services were "on-time". There were two pages of services shown on the board, and the only delayed one was a Cardiff service. However, one by one, all the services gradually changed to "Cancelled". Officials said that a bus service was being set up. Ideas varied regarding where the bus services were coming from. Some said they were to come from Wrexham, and some said Chester. The only clear point was that the busses were still at their point of origin, and any chance of progressing the journey seemed remote.

The station staff advised all passengers to make their own way to Shrewsbury. I phoned Clint and Darcie, near neighbours at Penybont, and they picked me up at 9:35, and drove me to Shrewsbury Station. Here, the platform electronic boards showed the onward train to Birmingham was cancelled. I went to the Customer Office and was told that the cancellation was because the crew was on the other side of the blockage at Chirk. I was also told that a herd of cows had been hit and that there was total carnage up there. I made a few comments about the availability of alternative trains and ability to cope with problems. They put me on a stopping train to Birmingham New Street. This arrived late because it stopped at all the villages on the way, including little halts.

At Birmingham New Street, I was told to get on the slow train to London Euston. It was a Northwest rail service, which also stopped at all the minor stations. Eventually the guard was replaced by an officious one who announced over the train intercom, that all passengers who had used the service after their travel problems, had to get off at Milton Keynes, or he would impose a £100 penalty, and in addition we would have to buy a new single ticket to London. I tried to reason with this jobsworth, but he was having none of it. He said we were all Avanti customers, not Northwest rail. His head was fixed so rigidly, that he didn't seem to care, or want to help those who had been through difficulty. I look back with fondness to the days of British Rail with a common ticketing system. Its logo seemed to indicate that it didn't know whether it was coming or going, but at least there weren't different companies pulling in different directions and refusing to help passengers get to their destinations. It would have been easy for the guard to have either taken note of the number of passengers involved, and to seek reimbursement from Avanti, or if he lacked the ability to do this, to simply overlook the situation on this occasion. All the inconvenienced passengers alighted as requested by the jobsworth guard at Milton Keynes, and were told to wait for the next Avanti service to London Euston. Messages over the Tannoy system revealed that this train was an hour late due to a "police incident", wording that is often used to cover a wide range of lateness issues. The train did eventually arrive and got to London Euston at 3pm.

Then I used the tube train to get to Heathrow. In the old days, you used to walk up the ramp from the Euston platform, cross the concourse and go down the elevator to the underground. Not now. It's been "improved". You have to walk outside, turn left and then enter the underground from outside. It wasn't raining at this point, but why can't they connect internally and make it better for everyone? The route I use on the underground is Victoria Line to Green Park, and Piccadilly Line from Green Park to Heathrow. Trains are frequent, provided the operators are not on strike.

When I arrive at Heathrow, I've always used a free bus to get out of the terminal. You have to use a vehicle. They don't allow you to walk out of Heathrow. Just why is a mystery. Many airports across the world are accessible on foot, but Heathrow is not. There used to be lots of busses that were free provided you got off after the first two or three stops. There are no free bus services now. You pay for the service, even though it's a few hundred yards. I took the 105 service to Cranford where I alighted, and walked the 1.5 miles to my accommodation, 37 Arundel Street, called Babus International. On arrival, there was nobody about, and the property looked like a semi-detached council house. The only thing that distinguished it from all the others nearby was a cloth notice outside the gate bearing the name "Babus International". I phoned the owner, who was somewhere else in the UK. He gave me the code to a key box on the outside of the property. The key from the box gave me access to the hallway. My room was upstairs and the key was in the door. The room was ok, with a shared bathroom on the upstairs landing. There was a bed, a dim light, a socket, and a window from which the Heathrow planes could be watched every 20 seconds or so, and heard a lot too.

By this time, it was 5:30pm, and I was feeling the need of something to eat. A couple were standing outside with portable fires attached to their mouths by white tubes. I asked if there were any restaurants in the area. They gave directions which I followed and came to a row of seedy establishments, and a large forecourt finished badly and with different patches of material. Several commercial vehicles of dubious quality were there providing cover for dubious deals to be conducted. I went in the café and ordered cottage pie, apple pie, and a mug of coffee. By the time I had finished, it was raining properly, which is the most common feature of British weather. It may be warming up as expected after the ice age, but it certainly is able to rain for lengthy periods here.

I walked quickly back to my digs and hung my jacket to dry. Then I mailed a few friends with the day's adventures and my boss, who is trying to resolve the fact that I have not yet been paid for shifts I worked in June. When I started in the NHS, things were very simple. You could still be paid in cash if you wished. A guy used to bring it round in little bags. Most of us had it paid into our banks. It was simple to work out. There were discrepancies occasionally; we accept that. You could ring up and it would be sorted promptly. To get a discrepancy sorted out now involves a number of steps. You can't just ring up the person who puts the money in your bank. You now have to go to your manager, who has to go to his manager, who has to go to payroll. Mails have to pass between them, and documents have to be signed, and it has to be proved that you have done the work for which you haven't been paid. Once all that has been mulled over for a few weeks, they will deign to pay you. If the discrepancy is greater than £100, they are meant to put it right immediately by a bank transfer. In my case they didn't bother until another month went by. I could have needed that money urgently to pay a bill. I know that if the discrepancy had been in my favour, they would have arranged immediate repayment from my next paycheque.

My attention turned away from these matters to consider my upcoming flight to Canada. I had tried to check-in online a few times, using the reference number on my flight documents. It was unsuccessful, and each time, the message came up telling me that I could not check-in until 24 hours before my flight. Now, it was less than 24 hours to my flight, and the same frustrating message came up. I went onto the Air Canada website and searched for information on my flight. I discovered to my consternation, that it had been cancelled due to a fault with the plane. I also found that Air Canada had put me onto an alternative flight, that would stop in Washington, and arrive in Toronto at nearly midnight. I installed a taxi app called "Bolt", and was able through that, to arrange for a taxi to take me to the airport at 03:00. I was hoping to arrange for an earlier flight in order to pick up my hire car, as pick up out of hours is not normally possible. At the airport, I found that nobody from Air Canada was available until 05:30, so I had no choice but wait until then.

At 05:30, the Air Canada staff informed me that the alternative flight through Washington was not possible because I did not have an "ESTA" (The USA entrance authorisation) card. They arranged the alternative of flying from Heathrow terminal 5 to Manchester, and then on to Toronto. The problem as I saw it was that the flight to Manchester left Heathrow T5 at 10:05 and left Manchester for Toronto at 12:05. This left only half an hour to make the connection between two different terminals at Manchester. This was of course a tall order on stilts. However, the Heathrow staff said it would be fine.

The next job was to get to Heathrow T5. The Air Canada staff told me to take the Elizabeth line express train to T5 and it would be free. I walked to the Elizabeth line station, which was quite a distance, only to find that there had been an "incident", and the line was closed until further notice. How many more "incidents" was I going to be subject to? Anyway, I had to walk all the way back to T2 and get the underground to T5 instead. I had no tickets to access the underground, so I managed to squeeze through two barriers behind another passenger. I didn't see another choice frankly, as it wasn't my fault that my travel situation was unravelling.

Once in T5, I had to find the check-in desk for British Airways (BA), who was operating my next flight. There was a queue of nearly one hundred people, and it was advancing extremely slowly. Many in the queue had excessive baggage and other issues, and it was two hours before my turn came. The lady at the desk was great and provided my boarding pass for the flight to Manchester, and my on-going flight with Air Canada to Toronto. She did say that I would have a job making my connection. The BA flight was half an hour late on arrival, and my Air Canada flight was due out as we landed. I had given up hope of making the connection. In addition, the only way of getting from T3 to T2 at Manchester is to leave flight side. This meant that I had to go through security again. There was a long queue waiting for the X-ray checks. I shouted my predicament across the queue and they called me through. A distant guard ran over and called me back. I explained the situation and he relented. The staff at Manchester security were slow and unhelpful. They wasted more time by testing my liquids in a chemical analyser. I explained that their delays were probably going to cause my connection to be lost, and they just didn't seem to care. The result was that I was an hour late when I arrived at gate 218 for my flight. They were all ready to go, but had kindly waited for me. I could have kissed that crew.

Even though, due to my late arrival, that plane was over an hour late leaving, it still arrived in Toronto at 15:15. To say I was made up would be an understatement. Were things starting to go right? Well, I hoped so, but there is a long process to get out of Toronto airport. There are four stages of security. The first one is electronic. You stand before a machine, and remove your glasses and hat. It photographs you and compares the image with your passport. It didn't like what it saw. I had to do it again. You then enter another hall and the same thing happens again. Then you go before an official who wants to know what you have come for and where you are going. Then you pass through a final check after which you are free to enter Canada.

I looked for signs to rental cars. None were visible. I asked for help, and was pointed in the right direction. Not until you've walked about a mile, and negotiated escalators, lifts and turns, do you find any signs with reference to rental cars. Eventually, I reached the car hire area and the Hertz desk was the last I came to. The official looked at my driving licence, and I was charged $1700 for a one-way surcharge, and a refundable deposit on the car. I thought I was finished and would be handed the keys to my car. How wrong I was. They sent me onwards to another office. There, they looked at my driving licence again, and my credit card, and gave me more documents to sign. What an inefficient time-wasting process this was. If one Hertz official looks at your driving licence, and credit card, why does that have to be done again twenty yards further on? I was picking up a hire car, which I had paid for in full, months ago. I understand that my licence had to be examined, and further charges had to be made, but are Hertz officials unable to do this in one go rather than have two guys doing the same job twenty yards apart. Then I understood the need to waste time. The car I had reserved had gone, loaned to a person who turned up on spec. There were no cars available, and I had to wait until one was returned. There was a gathering crowd of people who had been treated the same way, and they were getting increasingly upset to be told that there were no cars at present.

I called an official and complained, because this situation was out of order and unusual compared with all the countries and occasions when I have called to collect a prepaid vehicle. They found me one soon afterwards. It was a Nissan Versa, a model I had never seen before, and one which I soon called the Vice Versa. I walked around it and checked for dings, cracks and defects. All seemed well though visibility was awful in that underground dimly lit area. Some things immediately struck me about this car. Although modern, it did not have central locking. Visibility to the rear and side was poor. Never mind. It would hopefully be my means of traversing Canada, possibly my occasional bed, my protection from the elements, and if the scaremongers be believed, my protection from herds of aggressive wildlife.

All I needed to take

25th July 2023   17160 – 17280

Toronto to Niagara Falls

I fixed up my TomTom on the windscreen and plugged the lead into a USB socket on the dashboard. I entered Niagara Falls as my destination and asked for the route. It told me that no route was available. With all that had happened over the last couple of days, I wasn't thinking straight and began imagining that I was down to sheet maps and road direction signs. Then the fog cleared and I realised that my poor TomTom, and my car was underground. It couldn't see any satellites. I had just fished it out of its bag and plugged it in. As far as the dumb technology was concerned, it was still in Penybont, the other side of the Atlantic. No wonder it couldn't find a route. I gingerly emerged from the parking lot. There is no layby to sort yourself out in. You are immediately on the road with stuff wanting to charge forward at high speed. I just had to get on with it and looked for signs heading south. Then joy of joys, the TomTom must have realised that it was in Canada, and it started to give me directions. It led me off the highway and down side streets. Eventually, I found somewhere I could stop. I found that I had set the device to find the shortest route. I altered this to the fastest route. The TomTom got me back on the highway, and together, we made progress to Niagara.

    I found the Glengate Hotel in Niagara Falls where I was to spend my first night. I parked the car and checked in. I was allocated a nice room with aircon, microwave, fridge, a king size bed and a nice ensuite. Then I went to look at the Falls. How Niagara Falls had changed since I last visited twenty years ago! It was tremendously busy with every available parking area charging to stop. When I last visited, you could park on the streets easily and freely. Now the town is awash with entertainment, and is extremely busy and congested. The Falls had not lost their appeal and majesty. So great is the force of them, that you are in a wet mist half a mile away. The volume of water roaring down as Lake Erie empties into Lake Ontario, is amazing. Yet status quo is maintained by the water cycle as Solomon reminded us three thousand years ago when he recorded that the water runs into the sea, but the sea is not full because the place where it comes from, it returns to again. The force of water was so great that the falls were edging back towards Lake Erie at a rate of two foot per year. That has been reduced to a much smaller amount by the hydroelectric scheme downstream. Half of the Niagara River flow is ducted to the power station through three huge pipes. At night, when less electricity is demanded, the flow increases and this is impressive. Of course, it's dark, but they do floodlight the water with coloured lights. It isn't natural, but it looks pretty and folk like that sort of thing. The rainbow in the mist is as I remembered it. The noise of the water is much less noticeable today because of the vehicles and entertainment drowning it out. When I last visited, you could hear the falls from streets away. Now, the hooting of horns and the deep throb of thousands of Cummins diesel engines, are the main decibel contributors of Niagara. People have always been impressed by the falls. Most of us just stand and watch in awe. Some are moved to make arrangements to go over in a barrel. The first recorded is a lady who had herself and her black cat stuffed into a wooden barrel, wrapped in a mattress. She asked her assistants to nail the lid on. They asked, are you really sure about this? Yes, was the answer. They nailed it shut and pushed her off. It didn't take very long to get to the bottom where anxious aides fished the barrel out of the water and prised the top off. The lady and her cat clambered out fit and well. The next person to go over thought he would do one better. He procured a strong metal barrel and over he went. When they fished him out at the bottom, he was dead. He thought he was doing himself a favour by using a metal barrel, amply strong enough to endure the violent descent. What he had overlooked was that he would be rattled like an ice cube in a cocktail shaker during the descent without any padding. You've probably seen an enthusiastic bar tender doing this activity over his head with all his might. The only person known to have gone over the falls and survived unharmed, is a twelve-year-old boy. His parents got into difficulty in a small boat above the falls. The lad fell out and over he went. He was picked up completely unharmed at the bottom by the Maid of the Mist boat. His only protection was a life jacket, which quite possibly saved his life. There are lessons to be learned from all these things. The main one is that life is a wonderful opportunity. It's best to use it wisely, and not risk shortening it by a quick thrill. And, if you want to go boating, don't try it above a waterfall, especially a big one.

    Next came the need of a meal, and at the same time a large surprise. Canada is a nation of fast-food outlets, but few proper restaurants. You will seldom find a sit-down restaurant offering meat and two vegetables. There are such places, but they have to be searched for. There are the same fast-food outlets as in the UK, and a whole lot more besides. Many of these are drive through places where you order and pay at one window and advance forward to another window through which your wrapped grub and a can of gassy fluid is passed. Then you take this home and get fat on it. You'd expect that Canadians would have a short life expectancy, but it's longer than ours in the UK. Of course, there are other things to take into consideration. When you get ill in Canada, you are seen to right away. There is no waiting for months or years for operations and vital treatment. Yet, it was a surprise that the five a day lecture that is drummed into UK citizens, seems largely ignored in Canadian eateries. We all like fish and chips in the UK, which is a fry up, whose cancer-causing properties are enhanced by the amount of nuclear waste and shredded plastic that the fish is stuffed with. But we usually get it served with peas of mushy or garden type, and that makes it all right! In Canada, you don't get the peas. If you really want your five a day, you can sometimes ask for a separate side salad. Anyway, I got a "Subway" sandwich at a place by the Glengate Hotel. Then I walked to the nearby Chucks Bar for some liquid refreshment for medicinal purposes.

    Back in my hotel room, I made use of the excellent WiFi to contact loved ones back home. And, here's the thing. My network provider was sending me messages saying that I needed to buy an internet package from them to enable me to use my phone in Canada. EE and other providers must be sick of people avoiding these rip offs by using WiFi connections. When abroad, I turn my data and roaming facilities firmly off. People have got used to fishing their mobile phone out every few minutes to see who they can chat to, and what they are saying to them. I lack all that, but at least, I can happily be without communication all day, and just send a few photos to folk at night and use Google to book my next night's accommodation. The only thing is that Canada is between six and eight hours behind the UK, depending on where you are, as there are six time zones in Canada, though only four main ones. It's a big country, second in size only to Russia. Unless your folk at home are night owls, they won't receive your message until their morning, by which time, you will be out somewhere. The thing is with messages home to say you are having a nice time, frankly irritates people and makes them jealous. When things are going wrong, they get interested; even fascinated, but news of balmy days in the sunshine does nothing for them at home when it's cold and drizzling.

Horseshoe Falls Niagara

American Falls Niagara

Niagara River and bridge between Canada and the USA

26th July 2023   17280 – 18098

Niagara Falls to Sault Ste Marie

17.45l = $30.36 at 17483 at Onroute Barrie

16.96l = $28.81 at 17831 at Nairn

I checked out of Glengate Hotel at 05:30 before daybreak, as I had a long drive ahead of some 470 miles. The stars were out and a long haired black and white skunk was walking across the carpark in front of my car. Sadly, it disappeared before I could get a photograph. It seemed to be a good start as far as seeing the wildlife of Canada. The weather was warm and dry, but the car was covered in a heavy layer of condensation, and the air was misty. You could see it hanging in the shafts of light from the street lamps. Though warm, it had an autumnal feel. They don't talk about autumn here. It's called "Fall", which is a bit odd because nearly all of their many millions of acres of forest are pine trees, that are evergreen. The Fall applies to leaf drop from deciduous trees, which are in the small minority in Canada. Anyway, they call it "Fall" instead of Autumn.

I set off towards Toronto again, noting that though it was early, the roads were very busy. As I reached Toronto, there were four lanes in each direction, and all the lanes were fully occupied by dense traffic. I was glad to head north out of Toronto towards Sudbury, and notice the traffic thinning out. The road became a dual carriageway once clear of Toronto and the speed limit was mostly 100kph (60mph), though there we're long stretches limited to 90kph. I was determined to keep to the limits to avoid any problems, and it was easy to do so as my Vice Versa was fitted with cruise control. I didn't see any fixed speed cameras, but there were occasional police cars. Many of these were unmarked, but lit up with flashing blue and red lights when they intended to pull someone over. I hadn't gone far when I saw a lorry on the hard shoulder, whose driver was bent over while they were fitting him with a pair of handcuffs. I don't know what sort of misdemeanour results in being led away in handcuffs, but I intended to stay within the legislation.

I had two speed indicators in my car. I had the speedometer and I had my TomTom, which accurately derives my speed from the satellites. Both readings were close, though the car's speedometer was one or two kph higher the TomTom reading. It is normal for cars to overestimate speed, and therefore, I set my cruise control to the TomTom reading rather than the car. Even so, I was about the slowest vehicle on the road. All the cars, even those towing caravans and boats, and trucks, were tearing past. It seemed that the view held by Canadian drivers is that the police don't bother you unless you are exceeding the limit by at least 20kph. There is certainly almost zero respect for the speed limits, and very little patience with anyone trying to keep to them. Frequent roadside notices displayed the consequences of breaking the speed limits. These ranged from demerit points and fines up to immediate impounding of your car and licence suspension for more enthusiastic progress.

I spent most of the day driving through dense pine forestry, which was quite pleasant. The roads were mostly straight and distant horizons were an interesting feature as I continued through this vast landscape. Occasionally, I was close to the shore of Lake Superior, and the beaches were like being at the seaside. You looked out across the lake which was far too vast to see the other side. I was travelling on the north shore for hundreds of miles. The southern shore is in the USA. I stopped occasionally to look at the beaches and properties opposite the shore. Most houses in this area are wooden and surrounded by forestry. It struck me at the time that though these people are familiar with forest fires, they have taken no steps down the years to reduce the risk of fire and of property loss should fires break out. It doesn't take a lot of imagination to work out better strategies, but they've chosen not to. You would expect for example, to have fire breaks in the forestry of perhaps a mile wide to restrict fires to areas. You may also expect large clearings around property, not only to reduce fire risk, but to let in more light. I kept hearing news of forest fires affecting large swathes of Canada and northern USA, but I had so far seen no evidence from smoke or flames. I hoped that this would continue.

As I was driving past Sudbury, a truck came storming past me and cut in over a hatched area. Grit flew up and a lump hit my windscreen about four inches from the bottom. It cracked down to the bottom and curved round to the right and started spreading across the screen. I was worried about the whole screen caving in. The weather turned wet and miserable, and so did I. Though I have driven about one million miles in all sorts of vehicles, I have never had a broken windscreen, and yet here I was on my first day out with the hire car, with a crack spreading across the screen. I wondered what else was going to happen after the adverse start to my holiday. As I passed through each town and village, I kept an eye open for auto-glass garages. At the close of my journey at Sault Ste Marie, I found two. The first was on my left as I entered the town. The owner said that I needed a new screen, but that it would be five days before he could acquire and fit it. He directed me to another garage where I was told similar information, but the price of $950 for the job was given. Both garages provided comforting news that my screen would not cave in. Laminated screens don't do that, and the crack is in the outer layer, not the internal glass layer. I decided to press on with my journey for the present.

I called at my accommodation, the Ambassador Motel, and checked in, and then went out to seek a meal. I ended up at "Chucks" where I chose chicken breast with some salad. My earlier view, generated by my Niagara experience, that they don't seem to do proper meals in Canada was reinforced at Sault Ste Marie. My chicken was large, but excessively dry, and I had a job to get through it. Having achieved this feat, I returned to my digs to try and book accommodation further west. I booked at Thunder Bay for tomorrow.

My Vice Versa

Wooden property Lake Superior

Lake Superior

Lake Superior

27th July 2023   18098 – 18810

Sault Ste Marie to Thunder Bay

13.206l = $22.44 at 18099 at Niagara

23.607l = $41.76 at 18585 at Terrace Bay

I left Sault Ste Marie at 07:00 and followed the Trans-Canada Highway westwards with the goal of reaching Thunder Bay by mid-afternoon. Unfortunately, I hadn't factored in the major roadworks, which the Canadians call "Construction". I'll give the Canadians praise for the quality of their roadworks before I give you the negative points. In the UK, it is rare to drive down a road with a loose-fitting crown, or dentures and fillings. During the first mile, all that isn't welded to the chassis, has shaken loose and is rolling around in the footwells. Although the technology to provide the UK with even road surfaces exists, it isn't often used. The roads are full of big potholes and sunken drain and manhole covers. Services in the UK are run below the road surface. This includes gas, electricity, communication, water, and drainage. The normal manner of resurfacing is to spray the road with tar and then strew ballast over it. This faithfully reproduces all the road imperfections about one centimetre higher up. The drains and other service covers are not raised, and each time they apply the surface dressing, the services become successively lower and more damaging to your vehicle. Road schemes in the UK are usually unseen because they close the road for a day or few before the work and open it a day or few afterwards. Mainly this allows the workers to enjoy their sandwiches and tea in peace. They cite safety reasons for road closures. Of course, the navvies could get grit flicked into their picnic, and that wouldn't be very nice, but normally, their road closures mean miles of detours for the motorists.

This nonsense doesn't happen in Canada. Services do not run below the road surface, except where necessary in towns. Mostly, services run in channels at the sides of the road. They have tried the noxious practice of surface dressing in Canada, but its use is not widespread. They have many thousands of roadworkers in Canada on hundreds of schemes across the country. It is a major source of employment, and of course, disruption. Many of the projects take months or years to complete, but one thing is obvious, and that's the quality of the completed work. Road surfacing is performed by several massive machines that follow each other down the road. They don't tend to shut the road in Canada. They do one half at a time, and control the traffic with lights, or more often, flag waving comics at either end of the disruption. I use the word "comic" intentionally. These people are excessively bored as most of us would be after hours of flag waving. They relieve the boredom by dancing, waving and gesticulating to the traffic. The drivers seem to like this attention, and wave back. I know it isn't their fault, but personally, I find the holdup frustrating, especially when it is only one of many each day. Still, it's probably better to have people employed on something useful, than loitering around towns causing trouble in between going to the Post Office for their handouts. We slightly digress. The machines doing the roads in Canada start with a massive blowlamp that treats half the road at a time. This advances slowly down the road, heating it and softening the upper two inches. The next machine lifts that upper two inches and crushes it. Next, the crushed road is mixed with new asphalt as necessary and it is laid smoothly and large road rollers finish the job. In this manner, miles of road are properly resurfaced to a high quality every day. It is then left to harden overnight before the other carriageway is done the following day, or within the next few days. Long lengths of road are tackled in one go, which means that the queues building up are also miles long. You are often held up at these projects for half an hour to an hour, waiting for your turn to go through. You are supposed to go through the section under repair at 30kph, which is less than 20mph, and this takes some time. Most Canadian drivers can't wait, and will blast through when they think they can get away with it. The speed limit boards tell you that if you speed through roadworks, your fines will be doubled, but still, they roar through. At many larger roadwork schemes, they stop the speeding by making you follow a convoy pilot vehicle. This is one up from the early British system of making cars follow a guy walking down the road with a flag. At the end of the work, you are meant to go dead slow for another hundred metres or so until you come to a sign saying, "Resume Speed". By this time, most Canadians are disappearing towards the horizon in a cloud of smoke, with their 3.5l Cummins diesel engine on full chat.

Today was very misty when I set out, with poor visibility. I drove so that I could stop within the distance I could see, but those on autopilot, hurtled past. The mist lifted later on, and the rain gave way to warm sunny intervals. I stopped a number of times to look at the shore of Lake Superior. What a huge body of water! It is about 32,000 square miles. The size was brought home to me after driving past it for two days.

Towards Thunder Bay, a finished road scheme at Nipigon had a viewing platform, which I ascended to look at the new bridge to the east and towards Lake Superior to the south. An idea of the size of the road project is when a viewing platform is erected as part of it. I don't know how high the platform is, but there are over sixty steps of ascent.

I was glad to arrive at Thunder Bay, and find my accommodation, the Nights Inn Motel. I determined on this occasion to find a proper meal, instead of the fast-food offerings I had thus far seen. I found Lot 88, which seemed a strange name for a restaurant. I guessed it was the number of the plot on which it was built, but I don't know, and neither did anyone else seem aware of the origin. Anyway, my joy was complete when I spotted baked salmon with root vegetables, and mashed potatoes. They also provided broccoli with it. The portion was on the small side, accentuated by the huge plate on which it was served. It would have looked more if they had presented it on a saucer rather than a piece of crockery the size of a serving tray. But it was very nice.

I returned to Nights Inn Motel which was adequate, but there was no kettle or other water heating apparatus. Neither were there any coffee or tea bags. A friendly man in the next room brought me a handful of tea bags and a bottle of milk and told me that the motel owners had a supply of kettles for loan. I've never known this sort of kettle loan arrangement before, but there we are. Kettles in Thunder Bay are clearly a hard to come by item that require heavy policing. Importantly, I had a few cups of tea, wrote up the day's log, emailed a couple of folks in the UK and booked my next night's accommodation.

The window of my small, but adequate room, looked across a few yards of rough ground to the main railway line. Through the night, freight trains passed steadily, preceded by much horn sounding that ensured you were awake to observe the passing. These trains had between one and two hundred wagons, and had two engines at the front, one in the middle, and one at the end. It's good to see so much freight shifted this way, rather than by road.

Tree lined roads

Nipigon viewing platform

South from the viewing platform

Child's portion, adult price

28th July 2023   18810 – 19496

Thunder Bay to Steinbach

11.631l = $18.48 at 18817 at Thunder Bay

15.674l = $25.06 at 19160 at Dryden

I left Night's Inn in Thunder Bay at 6am, and couldn't help noticing that the traffic was already heavy. This Inn had good WiFi, but was basic in most other regards, though adequate for my needs, and had a comfortable bed. I left Lake Superior at Thunder Bay, and it was another day with fresh prospects, as I headed northwest, and I hoped all would go well. Hope is the quality that keeps the spirit bright, even when things haven't been so good. There is always hope that things will pick up. They did, but as is normal in life, things are a mixture of good and bad. If we had all good, it would not form our character. We have bad as well and it is the bad experiences that brings out our resilience; fortitude; our ability to cope. Hope has to be balanced with realistic prospects; otherwise, it can lead to being disheartened.

 A thing Canada could do with is laybys at scenic viewpoints. Occasionally, there is one at the right place but mostly, laybys are surrounded by trees and the wonderful view that you wanted to savour is a mile back down the road, and it will be a busy road that is hazardous to walk along. What Canada needs is to employ a tourist to decide where the laybys should be; not an oik with no empathy with beauty. In Canada, traffic is heavy for a country of its size, and you can't just pull up and start shooting. You can, but it causes all sorts of problems. Anger and hostility are two of them, and that leads to much hooting and aggressive manoeuvres that are at risk of causing accidents.

 I had heard that the Trans-Canada Highway was sparsely supplied with fuel stations. This turned out not to be the case. A car will easily cover four hundred miles on a tank full of petrol, and I never found gaps of more than one hundred miles between stations. This is so unlike the Australian Outback where you can run out of fuel if you aren't careful, and it is wise to carry a spare ten litre can full. In eastern Canada, you can fill your car and then go into the kiosk and pay for what you've had, like you do in the UK. As you go west, this option doesn't exist. You have to pay at the pump with your card, or go into the kiosk and pay the attendant before you fill. It seems they don't trust people in Canada. Of course, you can fill your car and drive off without paying in the UK. It happens sometimes, but there are cameras on the forecourt, and it isn't long before the police arrive at your property if you attempt such a horrible theft. In Canada, you have to guess how much you will need, and key that into the pump. Some companies take the amount out of your account, and later refund you for the excess amount. More commonly, they only charge your card for the amount you've taken. The pump usually comes up with a figure of $200 to put on your card. I always decline this figure and select the option to set a far lower figure, just a little more than it will take to fill the tank. After a few fills, you get a feel for how much the tank will take. I always fill to the brim because it gives you the most range if your next garage is shut or difficult to access, and it allows you to work out your consumption figure. Here in metric land, your hire car shows your consumption in litres per hundred kilometres. You have to calculate miles per gallon which is our time-honoured figure that most of us know the meaning of. Most people aren't interested. This is especially true of Canadians who just pour the fuel into their twelve miles per gallon pick up, and roar down the highway as fast as they dare. I have an interest in fuel economy and like to see how much I can get out of the thing. I do all the things you aren't supposed to, to get the extra few miles per gallon, and it works. If you aren't interested, I don't mind. Just do it how you want, and we'll both be happy. What I can tell you is that the flat-footed point and squirt merchant who had hired my car before me achieved 6 litres per hundred kilometres. The computer hadn't been reset before I picked it up. I gradually reduced that figure to 4.9, and that's a big difference.

Anyway, I set off from Thunder Bay and met the first roadworks of the day. The highway was closed, and a diversion had been set up. The TomTom kept telling me to do a U-turn, but I persisted with the diversion. Eventually, TomTom realised that I wasn't listening, and it came out of its sulk, and went with the new route. Once I got on the Trans-Canada Highway, all was straight forward, except for lots of roadworks about 20 miles apart. Convoy trucks were in operation at most of them and the holdups were between ten and twenty minutes each, adding about two hours onto my journey. They were blasting at each site to move lots of rock and widen the road.

I think the nuisance of roadworks of this size will always be with us in Canada. The workers apparently get an average of $70,000 per year each and there are thousands of them at it. Once the current raft of projects is completed, the workers will simply move to the next stretch of road and start again. Digging up the road and relaying it is like painting the Forth Bridge. It is perennial. The public simply have to put up with the nuisance, and pay for it in their taxes.

There were points of interest along the way. Mostly, this was the huge Ontario Forest, which employs about 186,000 workers. It is a massive industry providing timber for many uses, including building about 30,000 homes per year. There are no breaks in the trees. They inanely hope that they won't catch fire, even though they do every year. The government requires the tree fellers to plant two trees for every one they chop down. The fires burn millions of them every year, but somehow, they keep the supply and demand going at a sustainable rate. The fact that for a couple of months of summer, much of Canada has poor air quality due to the smoke, seems neither here or there. It's been this way for a long time. They blame it on climate change. The only ones who don't are those who stop to think about it, and those with that ability aren't the ones making the decisions, so status quo is maintained. A lot of people are getting mad about it this year, but they are regarded officially as protestors, and not listened to.

The next point of interest was a fox, trotting along the main highway. The traffic was roaring past and the fox and the vehicles seemed unconcerned and mutually uninterested. I stopped at a nearby layby and the fox immediately became very interested. It waited until it was safe and crossed the road and came up to me. It looked rather thin, but otherwise bright eyed and healthy. I guess it wanted food, which I didn't have in the car. In any case, you aren't supposed to feed wildlife here. They can fine you up to $25,000 for doing so. They cite two reasons for the ban. One is to avoid the wildlife getting too interested in coming close to people and hurting them. The other is that our food is deadly to wildlife in their view. Frankly, I don't see much sense in either argument. Animals and birds do look to humans for food, and it is possible to interact with them in a positive way. Of course, if you tried to feed a lion with a chicken, it might choose you instead, so you have to know what you are doing and be able to read the animal's body language. If you get between a mother and her young, you are asking for trouble, but following a few simple rules, it is possible to have wonderful interactions with wildlife, and there are many people who make a profession out of it. The second point is our deadly food. The thing I've already alluded to is that Canadian fast-food lacks some of the nutrients advised by the "experts", but it gets the average Canadian to 82 years, so it's unlikely to be deadly to wildlife. They feed animals in zoos and on farms anyway. Of course, you have to know what to feed things. A fox is largely carnivorous, so it isn't likely to want your cucumber sandwiches, but it would be happy with your KFC. I took a couple of photographs and Google lens later identified it as a Nova Scotia fox.

I was interested in the fact that there were few insects. As soon as you get out of your car in the UK, there are troublesome flies everywhere. I live in the global epicentre for muck spreading, which is flicked all over the fields along the B4396. Farmers round here keep their cattle inside, and the waste goes into huge lagoons from where it is pumped into spreaders which the tractors tow for miles to the fields. This is nectar to the flies and when you drive along that road, they hit your windscreen like the rain. You can hear them plopping against the glass, and they are mighty difficult to get off once they have dried. Yet, here in Canada, I had driven a thousand miles and the backs of the door mirrors and the windscreen were largely clear. It was nice to get out of the car and eat a sandwich without having to beat all the flies off. No doubt, the environmentalists would have a lot to say about this. Perhaps we've hurt the sky and made ourselves too warm, but I guess that if you flattened the forest and spread cow dung everywhere, you'd soon have a similar fly problem to Penybont. For me, I was happy to enjoy a relatively fly free zone.

Next, I saw a wolf. It came out of the forest, crossed the road, and entered the forest on the other side. There is the old riddle; why did the wolf cross the road. The correct answer is, to get to the other side. There was once a lady with a certain hair colour who asked a lady on the opposite side of the river who happened to have the same hair colour; how do I get to the other side? The reply was, "you are on the other side". Anyway, the wolf was about the size of a large dog. By large, I mean Great Dane size. It was light in colour; not white, but light grey. I didn't have time to photograph it.

You get the idea, or at least I did before I came, that Canada is full of herds of caribou, moose, elk, bison, bears and the like. Nothing could be further from the truth. You rarely see them. It's just chance happenings. They cross the road in front of you, but if you set out purposely to see these things, you'll find it hard to see anything. While I was in Canada, a bear safari company was fined $35,000 for putting out food to attract bears. So unusual is it for bear safaris to show you bears, this company had decided to make sightings more frequent by putting the attractant out at a post where the land rovers would pass. Of course, the company, and the visitors, and the bears were happy. It's likely that whoever pocketed the $35,000 fine was also happy. It's an ill wind that blows nobody any good. The unfortunate fact is that wildlife in Canada, like the UK and the world in general, is getting much rarer. Many species are on the verge of extinction globally, and many species have become extinct. Most of this is down to us. When I was a boy, the human population of the globe was 2.5 billion. It's now about 8 billion. The competition for habitat is so intense that most of it has been lost. In the UK, green areas are being converted to concrete at an unprecedented pace. It's the same story everywhere. There simply isn't the wild space anymore for nature to thrive, and it's only going to end in more tears if time continues in the current manner.

In Australia, there are differences, but the human effect on wildlife is equally dramatic. There aren't herds of caribou there, but the indigenous kangaroo is plentiful. You won't have any difficulty seeing them. There are millions of them. Koalas were also plentiful, but idiots in the government put a bounty on the heads of koalas and wombats and this got rid of most of them, and that's very sad. Hunting of animals in Canada is also sad, and takes its toll on numbers. There are many thousands of signs warning you of wildlife on the road. You rarely see them dead or alive. In Australia, there are large numbers of kangaroo corpses at the roadside. You don't see elk and moose dead at the roadside in Canada. They simply aren't common enough to cause that sort of issue. Of course, if you did drive into a moose at 100kph, your next of kin would be informed in due time, and your car would be recycled, A full grown moose is about 800kg and at least as solid as a house.

Next, I came to a time zone change. There is some interesting history here. My phone and TomTom magically changed from 8:05 am to 7:05 am. A man called Sandford Flemming put this international system together and it's stuck ever since. A lot of countries tinker with the time twice a year and call it "daylight saving". It's an awful nuisance and most people would prefer in the UK to have British Summer Time (BST) all the year round. The daylight you have doesn't change by our little time schemes. It's a matter of having the hours best suited to the available light, and most people would benefit from BST year round. One or two groups hate the idea. Schools in Scotland is one of the groups. They are worried at the little dears going to school in the dark. Of course, that's not the real reason for switching the time about. It would be the easiest thing in the world to start Scottish schools at 10am instead of 9am. No, the real reason for keeping GMT during the darker half of the year seems to be a financial one. It has been shown that energy use would be less if they left BST all the year round. Some countries like Cambodia, don't tinker with the time and it gives less nuisance to everybody. But here in Europe, we can't leave well alone. Anyway, here at the time zone, plaques illustrating the international time system were displayed

Occasionally the road rose to a higher level than the surrounding countryside. Here I could get an idea of the massive scale of the Canadian forest and the large number of lakes everywhere. I stopped by some of the lakes and the most common water birds were swans. I saw few other birds today apart from crows and birds of prey soaring above the road.

There were many towns and villages to pass through. The thing that was lacking were restaurants where you can get a good nutritional meal and a coffee. Yet, I did get a nice coffee at a very reasonable price at a Punjabi restaurant along the highway. There was lots of good humour from the owner. He did me "a deal" where I had a packet of biscuits and the coffee for a discounted price.

Fox on the Trans-Canada Highway

Eventually, I came to Steinbach, where I had accommodation booked for the night. I had difficulty finding my digs. My TomTom has the most recent Canada mapping that I downloaded just before my trip, but address finding isn't very good to be honest. I asked directions, and managed to find it. I checked in, and then went to a nearby restaurant called "Smithy's". Here I had roast turkey with mashed potatoes and vegetables. The portion size was small, as I have experienced in another frugal food establishment. Again, it was served in a piece of porcelain the size of a tectonic plate, whereas a saucer would have sufficed and made the mental contemplation of the meal seem better. My motel was called "Sleep Suite", presumably the name was intended to convey the idea that you would sleep sweetly during the night. For that to happen, they would have to do something about the sound insulation. There are one or two nationalities who cannot apparently hold a quiet conversation. A pair of humans with x and y chromosomes were conversing in the corridor outside my room until midnight. The volume they were using was hideous. My next room inmate must have had a hearing problem. He turned his television on full volume, and kept it there. He had a number of messages on his phone and answered them with his fog horn voice. He set his alarm for 4:30am, and got up and left noisily, and left the alarm ringing. It was still ringing when I gave up and rose, and left at 05:30. I rarely get much sleep, but this night perhaps takes the record.

Entering Central Standard Time Zone

Long roads

Lots of lakes – this one is Umber Lake

29th July 2023   19496 – 20148

Steinbach to Regina

21.029l = $33.42 at 19573 at Winnipeg

19.212l = $30.72 at 19976 at Whitewood

I rose early and went to the lobby of the Sleep Suite motel, where I had a continental breakfast, which was included in the price. I had a bowl of cereal and a cup of coffee. Perhaps they can afford this little luxury seeing that they have saved money on the sound insulation? I hit the road at 6am as it was getting light. The golden ball of the sun was huge as it started to rise in the sky. It was so beautiful.

    I stopped at a place deemed to be the centre of Canada longitude. I took photographs of the place and of the spectacular sunrise. It seemed an iconic spot, exactly half way across Canada. I was taught geography by a lovely man who lived to the ripe age of 96 with his genial and wonderful way of putting things across. His explanation of latitude and longitude was simple. You may have heard it before. The guys who go to shows on stilts wear clothes with vertical stripes to accentuate their height. People who wear horizontal stripes appear fatter, and people challenged in that direction tend to avoid such clothes. The education was, latitude fatitude, and longitude; well, longitude. The latitude gives you the north/south coordinate and you express this first in a grid reference. The longitude gives you the east/west coordinate, and these are the last digits of your grid reference. Latitude and longitude are global and can be read on any map. It's a simple system that has stood the test of time, and is used as coordinates on sat nav systems everywhere. People like something novel and they've gone fawning after a new thing called What Three Words. Everywhere can be defined by this new system, but it sounds inane. When you tell someone to find worm.waddled.hats, you get the idea. You have a laugh and walk away. You can't use What3Words to navigate on a map, you can't use it if you have no mobile signal, which in the UK, is probably the case. You can't use it if the website is down. It helps snooping because the site knows exactly where you are. It's like your mobile phone. If you have location switched on, which most of us do, because it puts identification on your photos, but it relays to those who want to know, your exact position to the very square metre. What3Words is dependent on spelling the words absolutely correctly and it is case dependent. Thus, it is prone to error. I've never use it, and people who do navigation with maps prefer the proper way of finding places, which is to give coordinates. The first two give you the square on the map and the others you get by inspection. If you are half way up a square, you give the third figure of your latitude a 5 and if you are half way across a square, you give the third figure of your longitude a 5. You visually split the squares up into tenths and give the best fit.

Anyway, I was at the very centre of Canada. Well, the absolute centre is said to be a nearby tree of great age. This isn't advertised and I cannot find reference to it, but the locals are emphatic that this is the case. I found great interest in this place. I had only been on the road for a few days, and I was already halfway across Canada. I needed to slow down as I had over a month to explore. It brings into focus how small our little world is. It's only 24,000 miles round the middle. People sail round it in three months. Here we are packing more and more people into the small chunks of land we have. Three quarters of the globe is sea. How long can this packing exercise go on? Governments are generating a lot of tax by policies leading to less carbon going into the atmosphere, but are we seriously considering the increase in population, relative to the land area we have? You can actually apply for a one-way ticket to Mars, but few would seriously consider the prospect. It isn't really viable, is it? We are the custodians of this lovely planet earth, and we need to look after it better.

I continued to Winnipeg. And thence turned left to go round the city to its southwest. Then I entered the massive central prairie. This is the home of Canada's bread basket. Massive tracts of land covered by wheat can be sharply contrasted with our little five or ten-acre fields in the UK. That is of course, the fields that have not yet been turned into housing estates, or railway lines or roads, or other non-farming uses that net more cash than growing crops. I saw other huge areas given to sunflowers, whose happy heads were reflecting the hot sunshine.

Further, there were large windmills harvesting the breeze that gently sweep across this huge area. I guess that strong winds frequently blew across the landscape. There is little in the way to stop them. Today, gentle breezes were pleasant, without ruffling anything. It was lovely. I took a few photographs of the expanse. They are nothing to look at, but the feeling generated by the wide-open space is wonderful. The big sky. The endless horizons. The same feeling comes on the Australian Outback, except there you can stand and take it all in on the highway, because there is hardly any traffic. In Canada, you have to choose your spot. The best way to enjoy it is to escape up a grit side road. There you can relax and absorb this vast space.

I stopped at Whitewood at a lovely café where I bought a coffee and cake. The owner happened to be a photographer. His work was displayed round the walls. He really had captured the feeling of the prairie. He included some views of the northern lights, which he said were often seen there. I can imagine that as it is quite far north. Winnipeg is rather cold in winter, the temperature frequently dropping to minus 40C. That's twice as cold as your deep freezer. I experienced minus 25C once in the UK and for a few days in Norway, but minus 40C is a quantum leap beyond that. You need a scarf round your nose and mouth to stop it hurting when you breathe.

I was held up at roadworks again. The Trans-Canada Highway was made of concrete, constructed from a huge number of slabs separated by expansion joints. You clack over them like the carriages on an old railway line. They use continuous welded rail now, but in the former days, there was the clackety clack as you rolled along. So, it is on the Trans-Canada Highway, but not for long. They are resurfacing it with asphalt. They are doing it in 12km stretches, and the job will take a nice long time before they move on to another project. They limit you to 60kph through the roadworks, which isn't too bad. Some road works are limited to 30kph. It seems like eternity, crawling along a straight section at that speed. Even though the speed was limited, there were accidents. A huge truck lay on its side, crumpled on the east going carriageway, with a lot of people stood round it. Only a few seconds inattention is needed for such a result. I'm afraid that inattention peaks at very low speed. At higher speeds, you concentrate more. Most of the trucks in Canada roar along on full bore. In this area, a bus pulled out in front of one, a month ago. There was a large loss of life, and that has led to the authorities reducing speed limits, particularly at intersections. Of course, the speed limit only works for those honouring it. If you are the type that simply belt through, then the speed limit is pointless unless it is backed up by cameras and heavy fines. I know someone who was doing 140kph in a 100kph zone. He was fined nearly $400. His license was not taken. For people earning good money, such a fine is not a deterrent. License removal is a big deterrent as are very large fines. I think 100kph in a single carriageway and 120kph on a motorway is enough when it's busy. If you are going to roar through with no regard for the limit, then you deserve to be penalised a lot. Almost all Canadian drivers on the highway ignore the limit. That was my overriding experience. In the town, the limit is usually 50kph, and they simply roar round you if you try to keep to it. They do the same on the open road, even if it means going over double lines to do so. If they fixed cameras up it would stop all this and make driving a less stressful experience. In the UK, the opposite is true. Many drivers travel at half the road speed and cause holdups and queues by their slow and inconsiderate behaviour. We have an accident rate half that of Canada, but the frustration of being made to go between 30 and 40mph on the open road behind queues of slow-moving traffic is stressful. I'd sooner have the get up and go behaviour of the Canadian drivers than the lethargy of the average UK driver who seems to try and make the journey last as long as possible. Yet, I'd rather have the happy medium where we all drive at the limit when it's safe to do so.

    I carried on to Regina, and to Motel 6, where I had booked and paid for one night's accommodation. I settled into my "King" room. Don't you think it should have been a "Queen" room in Regina? My room was very quiet and comfortable. The bed was extremely large, and you would really need two people to make it. You could easily lie on it crossways, and it could form a sleeping area for five people. There was no restaurant in Motel 6, but the staff suggested I tried the grey building opposite. It was Earls Kitchen and Bar. I had baked salmon. I paid $45 for the salmon and mash with a pint of cranberry juice. I gulped at the price, but you have to remember that our poor economy and exchange rate in the UK, is not Canada's fault. They have a strong economy in Canada and high wages that on average are nearly double the UK. Anyway, my meal and accommodation were lovely.

    So far, I had not experienced forest fires. I kept getting messages from the UK where people had seen alarming news of the fires, but, I had not yet smelled smoke, or seen any. I hoped that this would continue. Sadly, I was affected later on in my trip, but I'll come to that in due time. For now, the sun was strong and the sky clear and blue.

Centre of Canada south of Winnipeg

My windscreen crack was spreading at a couple of inches per day and was a constant worry. I tried to find a fitter online, and I came up with a firm called "Glass Masters" at Calgary. They could get a suitable screen for my car and fit it on Monday. I confirmed the booking for 4pm.

Sunflowers

30ᵗʰ July 2023   20148 – 20625

Regina to Medicine Hat

18.0471 = $28.86 at 20342 at Morse

I left Motel 6, Regina at 06:40 and headed west on the Trans-Canada Highway. It was some time before I cleared this large busy city and found a right-hand turn up a grit road, where I found the peace and quiet to worship and remember the sacrifice made by Jesus who gave His life for His friends. He gave His all for the benefit of others, and asked us to remember Him in communion.

I continued westwards, stopping occasionally to photograph the vast open landscape. Eventually, about fifty miles east of Medicine Hat, the scenery became gently rolling, with only small fields being suitable for crops. The rest was left as open grassland, some of which was grazed by cattle. The change was pleasant, and it was possible to see more distant higher hills. I was getting nearer to the Rocky Mountains. The dual carriageway had been predominantly given a 110kph limit, but this reduced to 80kph at intersections, and 40kph through the abundant roadworks.

You may wonder why a city would be given the name "Medicine Hat". We know what medicine is and we know what a hat is, but the two in combination don't seem to make much sense. Apparently, it comes from a legend of the indigenous tribe who were faced with famine. It's all mixed up with special bonnets and human sacrifice and such pagan things. You can read the legends in City Hall, and no doubt, entertain your views on the truth of these matters.

The railway line ran parallel to the road, but the hillier landscape, which is fine for roads, cannot be negotiated by trains weighing many thousands of tons. So, the railway twisted from one side of the road to the other as the builders sought the flattest route for it. The highway bridged it on several occasions. I saw no passenger trains; only freight, and lots of them. The usual format of a freight train is two engines at the front, one in the middle and one at the end. In between are approaching two hundred wagons. Freight haulage by rail is a big thing in Canada. It is not in the UK. This is not because road haulage is better. It's because the corrupt transport secretary in the early 1960s, had his fortune tied up in road haulage, so he sought to have the rail network axed. His move was successful, under the hand of Beeching, and the powers that be didn't twig what was going on until it was too late. The transport minister fled to Spain, where he lived out his days in exile. There was no extradition in those days. The Canadian freight trains are long, and I videoed a couple. It took four minutes for them to pass me. One had 170 wagons and the other had 155. They weren't trucks in our sense of the word, but were bogie wagons holding one hundred tons each. It makes sense to transport large volumes and weights of goods by rail. Not only does it keep the road clearer than it would otherwise be, it is much more efficient. Canada has not had its railways Marpled or Beeched, and goes forward to provide the best way of transporting freight, especially coal and oil.

I drove past a large potash mine. There was nothing to say that's what it was, but the large white mounds and white dust everywhere, gave the game away. The final indication was a road going to it called Kalium Road, Kalium being the Latin name for Potassium. Used as a fertiliser, it enhances crop yields. Its sustainability is questionable since when the mine is worked out, there is no more, unless it can be found elsewhere. People always want to maximise crop yields. Sustainability and environmental impact are usually of far less consequence to most people. If run off from treated land gets into water ways, "well never mind" is the usual stance unless someone important notices and starts jumping up and down. Anyway, the potash mine wasn't a nice spectacle, but I guess it works for now.

The only other vast country I have been to with big skies and open space, is Australia. I can now compare the two. Canada is far busier in the countryside. Australia is busy in the cities, but once you get rural, there is peace and quiet. In Canada across the prairie, you'd think you were miles from anywhere apart from the constant stream of traffic. In the outback, you can stop at the side of the road and look round and savour complete solitude, until the next vehicle comes along in perhaps fifteen to thirty minutes. Canada is a little larger than Australia, but has roughly a 40% larger population, and they seem to like driving a lot. Canada perhaps has more peaceful spots in the Yukon and Northern Territories, but I didn't have time to explore them. Indeed, I was forbidden to do so by my Hertz hire car agreement.

When you stop for a bite to eat, or even a drink, you are expected to tip. Tipping in Canada starts at 15%, and they like you to give 20% or 25%. I've never met this kind of policy before. 10% tips are the norm in the UK, if service is exemplary. Here in Canada, you are often asked to pay and award the tip prior to trying out the food. Of course, waiters look forward to sharing out tips that are a nice bonus on top of their wage. However, I feel that the percentages sought in Canada are out of harmony with the rest of the world, and should be reduced to normal levels. They should only be expected after providing excellent meals and service. The average waiter salary in Canada is around $30,000, that works out at $15 per hour, which is rather low compared with the UK even, and illustrates the problem. If you pay people a decent wage, then you don't have to rely on customer's generosity to make it up with excessive tips.

The hot day gave way to a thunderstorm in the evening, with almost continuous sheet lightning, that vividly lit up everything. Hopefully, the rain is helping to extinguish the forest wildfires, though lightning is good at starting fires apparently. Depending who you listen to, somewhere between 10% and 90% of forest fires are started by lightning. Others say that human behaviour has a much larger part to play than officially suggested. Smoking is very much practiced in Canada, and the number of smoking stubs I saw tossed out of moving cars were countless. People think that this doesn't matter, but the reality is that a discarded stub is still burning slowly, and given hot dry weather with kindling, it isn't long before these things take hold.

I had booked Baymont Motel for my night's stay which was a strange style of building. It had a sort of pillared brick structure, but the real building seemed to be inside it, as if someone had built a new building inside the acropolis. Once inside, the lobby was enormous and had a central feature built from large rocks like a waterfall. There were two restaurants and lots of bedrooms. Mine was a nice room with decent facilities. I had a meal in the Indian restaurant, and it came out cool. I asked them to warm it up for me, and instead, they made a completely new meal. I just like a meal to be hot when it comes out. They could have put it in a microwave for a couple of minutes and it would have been fine, but no, I had a new meal.

I went out to check my car before retiring, and a rabbit was hopping round the car park. It seemed unconcerned, and I was able to get close to take some photographs. In contrast, the rabbits in the UK are very nervous, and are away at the first sign of human approach.

I tried to use Booking.com to arrange my next night's accommodation in or near Calgary, but my payment was declined. I tried again using a desk top computer in the motel, with the same result. The reason is because the WiFi network used by the motel is "insecure". This means that unscrupulous folk are able to hack in and obtain your personal and payment details. I used Expedia instead just for this night. I'm only mentioning this because if you need to book over an insecure system, that's the difference between Booking.com and Expedia. Both agents have access to the same or similar accommodations and prices are usually the same. Booking.com is a useful platform to check accommodation availability, and make bookings. Provided you review your bookings after you leave, you get discounts from future bookings. It works very well. Accommodations are in a cleft stick. If they use Booking.com, they have to pay a percentage of the booking for the advertisement and handling. If they don't use Booking.com, they miss out on a large percentage of the customers. It is possible to book and pay online, and this is the best strategy. Watch out for the small print. In New Zealand and Australia, there is a booking price and that's the end of the matter. In Canada, they tell you the extras in the small print. There are taxes, cleaning and service charges, which in a lot of cases double the room cost. Some owners would not allow Booking.com to accept payment beforehand. They wanted you to pay on arrival. I asked why, and was told that some of them had difficulty in getting paid by Booking.com afterwards. One was cross that I had got their accommodation so cheap with Booking.com. The thing is, I never paid less than the agreed price, but you know what you are paying if you do it beforehand online. In the accommodation lobby, they can charge you more if you aren't watchful. Most owners are fine, but there are some who are less fair than others.

Big sky on the way to Medicine Hat

Rolling scenery approaching Medicine Hat

31st July 2023 20625 – 20954

Medicine Hat to Calgary

20.846l = $29.16 at 20736 at Brooks

I rose at 5:30am and had a breakfast provided by the Baymont motel. There was cereal, fruit juice, coffee, fruit and yoghurt, and it was all good. I checked out at 6:30am and took the Highway 1 west.

The scenery was flattish prairie again for about 150 miles. I stopped from time to time to take photographs. One of these stops was to video another freight train. All the trains seemed to be freight. I hadn't seen a single passenger train from the highways. There are passenger services through the Rocky Mountains, and plenty of local services around major cities, and they are generally electric. Out in the wilds, the rails are used to convey freight between major cities, and especially to the ports. Some of the freight trains are shorter and they only have engines at the front and rear, but most are huge with a central engine for additional power and effectiveness.

I noticed many nodding donkeys today, whose purpose I had no idea. Initially, I thought they were pumping water for crop irrigation. Little did I know that Canada had a large number of successful oil wells, whose liquid gold was pumped by the nodding donkeys. Though small wells, many of them have been working very effectively for a quarter of a century. The fact is that Canada is third in the world for oil reserves, and is completely self-sufficient. This takes Canada out of the tyranny of states who get together to fix oil prices and hold much of the world to ransom. Canada can set its own price, and, as said, the price varies a lot with east Canada being very cheap at about 80p per litre, to more expensive in the west at about £1.20 per litre. Such low prices compared with the UK, together with comparatively high income, explains why little attention is given to fuel economy. For my part, I was pleased to have relatively cheap fuel for my long journey across and around Canada.

The landowners are doing rather well with these mechanical devices nodding away in their fields, surrounded by other crops. It's a rather different situation to the UK where landowners know that there's one thing that nets a lot more money than growing potatoes. Building land brings one million pounds per acre. I'm told that an acre of potatoes realises about £30,000. Therefore, you'd have to farm that land for 30 years to get your million back. The decision is made loud and clear. Farmer sells land for building whenever possible. This explains urban spread across our green and pretty landscape. It's a great pity. As farmland gets sold off, there are less farm jobs and all these countryside homes represent one or two cars on the road every day for miles, conveying the occupants to work, shops, schools and other things. The home is only a place to sleep. It's a thoroughly bad situation, but that's where we are. Births and deaths in the UK more or less match.

The increase in population is almost entirely due to immigration, and successive governments have allowed this to happen in a fairly uncontrolled manner for decades. The UK population was about 50 million in 1960, and about 70 million people now, that they know about. The UK has an extremely high population density, and pressure on green land is continuing apace. The situation in Canada is the opposite. The UK has about 280 people per square kilometre compared with only 4 in Canada. Well, there we are. The facts are available for all to see and for those in power to act upon, but the evidence is that nothing useful is being done to stall the population increase in the UK.

There is property development in Canada outside cities, but driving across Canada brings the assurance that there is still a huge amount of open space and green land. Many homes are built from wood, which is a renewable resource. Wooden homes can be long lasting if the wood is properly treated, and they can be warm and comfortable. Of course, the problem with wooden homes is that they catch fire easily. In the UK, we get a lot more rain than we used to, and a lot more flooding. Many homes are built and still being built in flood plains. The problem is one of getting property and contents insurance. It's the same in Canada if you have a wooden home near the forest. There is a fire risk rather than a flood risk, and your insurance is hard and expensive to come by.

I tried a few grit roads. The main highways are fast, but busy. The grit roads are peaceful and give the opportunity to really enjoy the landscape, and the freedom to get out and enjoy the sights and sounds of nature. You are occasionally disturbed by a pickup truck bouncing along at high speed in a great cloud of dust and debris, which takes about ten minutes to settle. Apart from that, the road is yours. Sensible progress can only be made slowly as these roads have horizontal ruts milled into them, that shakes the car and you at speed. You try and nurse the car along at about 50kph and all is well. I was impressed with the vast open skies. I was able to enjoy a paved minor road into Calgary for about 40 miles, and this was a nice alternative to the highway.

I eventually arrived at 10:30 into an incredibly busy traffic situation, with drivers seeming to be extremely impatient and throwing caution and rules to the winds. I made my way to Glass Masters where my windscreen was to be replaced, and checked that my new screen had arrived. Having checked that all was well, I drove to a shop and obtained sandwiches for my lunch, and then drove to a park by the Elbow River. I ate my lunch, read for a while, and had a nice long walk through the park and very wealthy neighbourhood. The houses were several million dollars each, sitting in beautiful gardens, many with the river at the bottom of the garden. This was obviously where the kings and queens of Calgary live. It was very quiet and peaceful, despite being close to the centre. You could walk into the centre from here, and indeed, this would be most sensible. Parking in the centre is very difficult and expensive. If you think you've found a place where you can park for free, your car will probably have been towed away by the time you return to it, and if you can find the company responsible, you'll pay a king's ransom to get it back. That's how it is in Calgary and some other Canadian cities.

At 2pm, I drove back to Glass Masters, and happily, they were able to get on with my car immediately, and at 4:30pm, it was all done, and I was on my way. I had two tapes fixed to the top of the new screen with instructions not to move them for 24 hours. I was also advised to leave a window open a crack and to shut the doors gently to avoid internal pressure that could lift the screen and lead to leaks. I'd never thought of the car as a pressurised capsule, but there we are. These people were giving sound advice, and I determined to keep to the instructions. The only pressure I've experienced is when a difficult person is sat at the side of me, barking, chiding and giving grief for the whole journey. There's no escape. I was on my own and the only voice I was subject to was TomTom lady telling me to make U-turns when I'd gone wrong. I paid the bill, which worked out to £404.20. I didn't think this was bad. The thing is that cheap little cars like mine don't have straight forward windscreens now. They have technology built into them to keep you on the straight and narrow. My windscreen included camera technology. The technology in mine was rubbish. It lacked the ability to drive the car for me. It just vibrated the wheel when you went over a white line and made some loud bleeping noises when you got too close to something in front. When there was no line at the side of the road, it would happily wander off into the undergrowth. Its lane control functions weren't worth having, and I'd much sooner not have these gimmicks. After all, you learn to drive and pass your test. You aren't going to climb into the back seat and do sudoku puzzles while your car smashes into things. No, you are going to look after it, and nurse it, and avoid the other idiots doing mad things. You are going to use your talent and arrive safely at your destination.

Anyway, my accommodation was a B&B called the Cozy Nest. It happened to be in a nice part of Calgary overlooking the River Bow valley, on the far side of which was the Olympic winter games park. You could see the ski slopes from the house. The delightful owner had responded to calls for accommodation for the 1988 Olympics and had maintained her property ever since as a B&B. She was a charming host, supplying lots of information about the area and its history. It was a lovely comfortable stay. I must have been tired as I got my little case out of the car and could not find my car keys anywhere. I searched all my pockets, bag, footwells, boot to no avail. Eventually, I asked the man staying in the next room to me for help. You've got it. The keys were in the car door lock. You get so used to central locking that when you have a vehicle without it, and are tired, you are apt to forget. Well, I did anyway.

I walked to a pub a few blocks away for an evening meal. It was very warm and humid, but much fresher for the walk back as it was getting dusk. I had a nice comfortable night, and would recommend this accommodation for anyone staying in the Calgary area.

American Robin

Across Bow River valley to Winter Olympic ground

1st August 2023   20954 – 21227

Calgary to Banff

14.1821 = $20.98 at 20979 at Calgary

Verna, the owner of Cozy Nest, cooked a lovely breakfast, included in the price. Set up for the day, I left at 08:30, and headed towards Banff.

My first real view of the Rocky Mountains was provided on Scott Hill summit. There is some controversy over the highest point on the Trans-Canada Highway, but this is said by many to be it, at about 1240m above sea level. Heights are a funny thing. The tide goes up and down, yet we always talk about sea level as if it were a fixed datum. The calculations are complex, and they use a mean point. The art of mapping, surveying and cartography, is an amazing subject. We can look at old maps, developed by the early explorers, long before modern instrumentation. They were amazingly accurate. The height of Everest was determined in 1847, many years before Edmund Hilary and Norgay Tensing bothered to walk up and have a closer look. We have known much about our little world for many years. Yet, we don't seem to have the sense to look after it very well, or to get on with one another. Up here on Scott Summit, I filled my lungs with fresh air and diesel fumes from the passing traffic. I don't want to spoil your mind's eye, but we may as well be honest about these things. As a child, I dreamed of seeing the mighty Rockies, and now that dream was fulfilled. In those far off days of childhood, there would be no traffic up here, but now there is; a constant stream of it. Similarly in the UK, few people had cars in the fifties. I lived in Wolverhampton on a main road. It was a single carriageway then, and the only car within sight was a shop owner who had an Austin A40 with large chrome hub caps, that got polished after every trip. Now every house host one, two, or three cars. Such major changes have occurred in our lifetime. Yet the Rocky Mountains haven't changed, and here I was looking at them. It was wonderful.

I had hoped on my visit to see all the wildlife as well as the mountains. An "expert" told me that I would need bear spray, and I would need to be very cautious about getting out of my hire car. I half expected to see an abundance of caribou, elk, moose, and bears roaming around in groups. They have laughable collective nouns for these things. The one for bears is a "sloth". Seeing that black bears can do 35mph for a while, the noun seems incongruous. Anyway, my first view of the Rockies did not reveal any of these animals. I hoped that would come later, as indeed it did. Don't listen to the wild tales. They are said for effect mainly. Don't get the idea that round every bend, the bears will be waiting to get you. Bear encounters are incredibly rare as black bears are declining in number and are extremely shy. One guide told me that he had to frighten a bear away by banging pots together because he came round a bend and saw a man sitting his daughter on its back in order to take a photograph. A believable tale? No, not at all. You might get to sit your daughter on a donkey, but on a black bear? I don't think so. It would be gone long before you had the chance.

Whatever wildlife you are privileged to see, savour the occasion. Make it known that you don't approve of banging pots at these animals, or shooting them. We should value our wildlife and enjoy such interactions as are possible. In my experience of looking for animals, snakes, birds and such like, they are afraid of humans with good reason. No creature has snuffed out so much life as the human being. Wildlife usually has better senses than we have, and spots us long before we spot it, and it slowly and silently withdraws from the area.

Today, there was hardly a cloud in the sky which was an intense blue, contrasting sharply with the snow and rock of the mountains, creating many picture postcard opportunities. I happily snapped away all day. Mountain lakes glistened in the sunshine, and the very gentle breeze did not ruffle their surfaces, but allowed them to perfectly reflect all that they saw.

I drove along the Trans-Canada Highway for another 40 miles before turning off into Banff. The scenery was somewhat similar to the Alps where I have seen snowy peaks, glaciers, canyons, and rapids in the past. Here was all that on a grand scale. The regular avalanche warnings seemed superfluous today, but winter would bring metres of snowfall, and a risk of these events. Today was calm, serene, and stunningly beautiful. I stopped for several short walks of a kilometre or so. One such walk was to visit Hoodoos, which are rocky pinnacles, that look like massive open-air stalagmites. They stand over one hundred feet high. Many signs told me to beware of bears since it was berry time. The berries were very nice, being a tasty blueberry. No wonder the bears like them. I did too. There were signs telling me to look upwards to notice the red squirrels. There were none of them either, although they are relatively abundant and can be seen in some parts of Canada.

I moved on to a couple of cascade walks where beautiful waterfalls could be seen despite the current dry weather. Much of the water in the cascades come from melting snow higher up, and is not influenced that much by rainfall or lack of it. There were a few people at the waterfalls. Some were sightseeing while others were shuffling about near the rivers. I think they were looking for fossils.

I had intended to travel down to Radium Hot Springs, but I had learned that hot springs could not be seen coming up through the ground. They had all been tamed and had swimming pool complexes built over the top. You pay your money and go into a manicured setting and sit in the warm water. You have no idea whether the warm water is out of the ground, or warmed by a boiler in one of the buildings. For my money, I'd like to see the hot water bubbling up through the ground. In the absence of a natural spring setting, I decided to enjoy the mountain scenery instead.

I drove to my accommodation in Banff, which was a hostel. Motels and hotels in Banff are prohibitively expensive. Such huge prices are only possible because tourists are prepared to pay them. I take the view that a couple of metres of toilet paper, a bar of soap, and a bed for the night, and the cleaning and resetting of the room afterwards, might cost £60 to £70, including staff salaries. When they charge £500 for this service, I don't pay it. If nobody paid these prices, it would quickly come to an end, and more realistic, and more friendly prices would prevail. Staff salaries and toiletries are no more expensive in Banff than anywhere else, and neither should the accommodation be. I was allocated a bunk in a six-bed dormitory. To say creature comforts and privacy were frugal would be an understatement. Five of the bunks were taken, and the only remaining one was a top bunk, which was accessed by climbing a creaky ladder. I explained to my room mates that I had to get up once in the night, and may disturb them. They did not seem bothered by this news. There was a nice communal kitchen and bathroom, and there was a restaurant and bar on site. I ordered fish and chips. Peas or vegetables were unavailable, but I paid extra for a side salad. The battered cod was about the size of a fish finger. The whole meal had a price tag of $33, and a pint was $7. Anyway, it was fine, and seeing that my growing days are over, it was probably adequate. The view of the mountains from the balcony of the restaurant was lovely. Staff told me that the black bears wander in the grounds. I assumed that the beer must be on the strong side since the forms wandering in the grounds were human. Bear spray was selling like hot cakes in the lobby, fuelled by the alarming tales and pictures around the place. It was provided in black canvas bags with shoulder straps. I carried a water bottle instead, which was of far more use to me in the lovely hot weather.

The hostel is called Hi Banff, and is absolutely fine, and cheap at $50 for the night, but for me the comforts and privacy of a nice room with ensuite facilities is nice. The whole area from Banff through to beyond Jasper, is singled out for great expense, especially for accommodation. My advice is to rough it in a dorm, or do what I did on other occasions, and that's to sleep outside the area, and commute in for sightseeing. It's a long way to drive, but a fill up of petrol costs $30, not $400 to $500 for a room. The other thing is that while you are driving along, you might see interesting things. The only thing you see in a hotel room is sheeting, curtains and walls. I did stay another night in Banff much later on in the trip, but that's another story.

Rocky Mountains west of Calgary

Bighorn sheep

Numa Falls

2nd August 2023   21227 – 21881

Banff to Rocky Mountain House

13.657l = $20.20 at 21229 at Banff

13.342l = $20.00 at 21536 at Jasper

I rose at 6am and set off from Hi Banff at 6:30am. I had heard that the bears are about early, and my son had been to Jasper recently and seen them at this time. I didn't even see any bear pooh. The right name for this substance is "scat", a dollop of which tells you that they've been in the vicinity, and you can tell by the look of it whether it's been recent or not. An inch on my sheet map is 64 miles, and it's easy to underestimate the distances involved. I planned to drive to Jasper, and then return to the Saskatchewan River Crossing, and then turn left to Rocky Mountain House for the next night, where I had booked accommodation.

It was a long journey to Jasper, punctuated by many stops to take in and photograph the stunning scenery. Some delays were imposed by roadworks, the longest being at a bridge construction site called The Big Bend. This was an appropriately named place for once as the road is in the form of a big bend to avoid the much more direct route which would cross the river and head straight upwards. In Canada, they always take a meandering route to ensure gentle slopes. They talk about steep winding roads. They need to visit UK mountain passes like the Wrynose and Applecross before talking about steep. The maximum gradient on a Canadian road is about 10%, whereas a mountain pass in the UK is often 25% or even 33%. The problem is, you wouldn't get an eighteen-wheeler up them, whereas they easily cope with Canadian passes.

At The Big Bend, some Bighorn Sheep were on the road. Some thought they were goats rather than sheep, and indeed, they had the goat look about them, but some locals in the know, identified them as Bighorn Sheep, as did Google Lens later. There was a layby from where they could be enjoyed safely. The scenery was magnificent, as was the intense blue sky and sunshine, which lit everything up so beautifully. Apart from the Bighorn Sheep, no other large wildlife was evident, which was a bit disappointing. My expectancy wouldn't have been raised except for the tales of great herds of beasts roaming about and all over the road. The expectancy was further heightened by loads of signs everywhere warning you about the wildlife and tersely telling you the fines to expect from feeding it.

My longest stop today was Columbia Icefield. Here you used to be able to walk up to the Athabasca Glacier. You still can walk up the mountain to where the glacier used to be in the 1990's, but the actual glacier is a bit further on, and they won't let you go there unless you pay for a guide. I'm always unwilling to fund rackets, so I photographed the spectacle from the barriers.

The alternative racket was to get a lift in one of about twenty coaches taking it in turn to ferry fifty people at a time up to the glacier and back. I watched the toing and froing and the queues waiting for their lift in amazement. There was a suffix to the venture where the coach would take you a mile further up the highway to a glass shelf on which you could stand or lie with a huge drop below you. The whole Fred Dibnah experience would be savoured with hordes of others for a total sum of about $130. I felt much more part of nature by walking up to near the glacier on my own.

The thing of note on the walk was a stiff cold wind coming downhill. This is called a Katabatic wind. Air striking the glacier cools significantly and falls as a result, and you feel it in your face all the way up. The other thing is the green colour of the torrent coming away from the melting glacier. The slowly moving ice has captive rocks which rub on the underlying sock and create a fine powder that they call flour. It is the suspension of this flour in the water that imparts its beautiful green colour, distinguishing glacial waterfalls and rivers from those supplied mainly with rainwater.

I was rather warm when I got back to my car, and it was like an oven inside. I was glad of the aircon and a drink of water, even though the water was warm. Soon after the icefield, emergency vehicles started coming from the west and hurtling by. It was clear that there had been another accident. Accident rates are measured in the number per hundred thousand drivers per year. In the UK its 2.7, but is 5.8 in Canada. They just drive like mad, and that's the difference. In the UK, they mostly drive like twigs in a brook at somewhere between the speed of tectonic plates and snails. When they bump into each other there is often no damage. They just get out, scratch their heads, exchange details and carry on. In Canada, a bump has usually written all the vehicles off, and imparted serious defects to the occupants. You can tell how many injured are expected by the number of ambulances on their way to the scene. On this occasion I only saw two, and two fire engines, and four police cars. Presumably there were two vehicles so that they could have an ambulance and fire engine each. The purpose of the fire crews is to put the vehicles out if they are on fire. If not, they have kit to open up the vehicles to get the occupants out. The purpose of the ambulance crews is to assess the injured, patch them up, and get them off to further care as soon as possible. The purpose of the police is to marshal the queues and carry out retrospective assessment of the scene to determine who did what.

I reached Jasper and filled up with petrol and set off on my return journey. When I reached the national park toll booths, I was told that there was a major accident ahead, and to obey the officials at the scene. I was told to expect a long delay. After 60km, I arrived at the scene in time to see them loading the scrap metal onto a couple of trucks. I was able to pass the site with hardly any holdup, which was a relief. These events serve a salutary lesson to drive carefully, observantly, and to the conditions. There is a subtle difference between this and driving slowly. A lot of people think that slow driving is good driving. It just isn't. Slow driving, with a queue of irritated people behind, is a recipe for unwise manoeuvres. You see lots of people driving slowly in the UK, wearing metaphorical blinkers, oblivious to the goings on outside their cockpit. They cause a good deal of nuisance. Talented drivers aren't slow. They have experience and use it to judge the best strategy on a continuous basis along their route. The object of a journey is to arrive at the destination safely, efficiently and courteously. If we could all do that, we'd save an awful lot of stress, expense, and time.

From Jasper, my journey to my accommodation at Rocky Mountain House was 285km, and the total journey of the day was about 600km, which is why with stops, I was out for 12 hours. As you will be noting, Canada is a big country. There is a lot more to a good trip than driving along the highway. The enjoyment is gained from stopping, walking, and appreciating the sights, sounds and smells of the environment. Most of the highway limit today was 90kph, at which speed, I was holding nearly all the traffic up and causing frustration. I'm afraid that I adopted the safer strategy of keeping with the traffic flow at 100 to 110kph to avoid causing trouble. An upside-down vehicle at the roadside, wrapped in police tape, demonstrated how unsafe driving could be in this place. It isn't just a matter of driving well yourself. It's much more a matter of avoiding those who don't. Driving with the flow, is the safest strategy on some of these roads.

Once I reached Saskatchewan River Crossing, I turned left towards Rocky Mountain House., which was only 100 miles away. My disappointment was that I soon left the Rocky Mountains behind. Rocky Mountain House is a large town, but its connection with the Rocky Mountains is only that you can drive to them from it. You can't see the mountains from the town; they are too far away. It's a false sense of identity really, and they should change the name to Not Rocky Mountain House, or some other name indicating the mountains were distant like Rocky Mountain Not Here House.

I reached Rocky Mountain House at 6pm, but had great difficulty finding my accommodation. The Voyageur was the name of my motel and I tried the name and the address. TomTom led me down a grit track to an area of rough ground, and told me that I had reached my destination. It didn't snigger at me, but it wasn't helpful. Either the motel no longer existed, or the data had been entered wrongly on the TomTom database. Unfortunately, the area of Rocky Mountain House I was in was mostly populated by immigrants. There was a large language barrier. Though I stopped and asked a few people, they didn't understand me. Even in the restaurants I went into for help, the staff could understand if you pointed to a menu option on a bill of fare, and they know what dollars are, but to supply directions in English was beyond the scope of their literacy. This is no criticism; I'm just stating my difficulty. I eventually found my motel by accident. It was set back from the main highway, but its name board was fixed high up, so I could read it from the road as I drove past. The accommodation was clean, pleasant, and quiet.

I went to a nearby grill for an evening meal. There were only fast-food places here. I asked for a side salad to supplement my chicken and chips. I looked round the busy venue, and I appeared to be the only one with a salad. Everyone else was gnawing their way through steaks. Afterwards, I returned to my motel room to read and write. The aircon was a nice feature as it was a hot evening. There is a large temperature range during each day. In the mountains, the day had started off at 4C, but by noon it was hot and now in the evening it was warm at 27C.

Rocky Mountaineer train at Banff

Athabasca Glacier

Athabasca Glacier

Endless Chain Ridge

3rd August 2023   21881 – 22154

17.78l1 = $24.15 at 22153 at Rocky Mountain House

I was out on a limb at Rocky Mountain House, where I had booked two nights. I decided to have a restful day with a drive into the middle of nowhere, to see what wildlife was around away from the main highway. I travelled along road 40 which is a long cross country unpaved route of varying quality. It was safely navigable at between 50 to 60kph. Any faster, you felt the car wandering on the loose surface.

Far from being in the middle of nowhere, the length of road I travelled on was given to camp grounds. The facilities are rudimentary, but people like to come out here in their huge camping vehicles and enjoy the Canadian outback. Every now and then, one of these vehicles, or a pick-up truck would roar by in a huge cloud of dust and debris. There were hundreds of Winnebagos, trucks pulling small house sized boxes on wheels. Many of these combinations towed smaller 4x4 vehicles on A-frames, so that after parking up, they had a smaller vehicle for local work.

The route I was on sported many boards declaring it to be a wildlife corridor. Really? Yes. They think that the creation of a road will provide a fast route for the wildlife to get from A to B. Wildlife doesn't think like us. It lives to eat and reproduce. Throughout my trip round Canada, I saw wildlife crossing the roads, but not using them for travel. The road is not a wildlife corridor, but a corridor for traffic. I drove about 100 miles on these grit roads today and did not see a single animal. Wildlife has sense regarding its needs. Herbivores want vegetation. Carnivores want catchable small animals. Neither is available on the road. The road offers a hard gritty surface, with danger and clouds of dust. If I was an elk, I'd give it a miss and get off into the undergrowth.

The day had started with a little drizzle, but by lunch time it was bright and sunny, and there were lovely views. I went for a walk and saw lots of clouded sulphur butterflies, and many grasshoppers that were jumping ahead of me. I saw no birds of prey. In the UK, country walks usually have buzzards and other raptors wheeling overhead, but here, there were none.

I eventually came out on the main highway between Rocky Mountain House and Saskatchewan Crossing, at a place called Nordegg, and drove back to Rocky Mountain House for the night. I had an evening meal in the Coop Supermarket. This seemed like a good option because you go to the servery and pick your fast-food options, which are presented to you in a box that you take to the till and pay for like your groceries. There are no tips expected. You just pay for the food and sit down, and eat it. They even provide disposable wooden cutlery to handle it with. I'm not sure how environmentally friendly wooden cutlery is. I'd have thought stainless steel reusable items would be better.

I sustained my first injury of the holiday at the Voyageur Motel. There were two double beds in my room, connected by a fixed shelf with sharp corners that was in the way whenever you got out of bed. You've guessed it. My nightly trip to the bathroom resulted in an inch of skin off my forehead and a trickle of blood. I have no early warning as I'm bald. It was wood to wood, and the shelf won. The wound dried quickly but left a nasty looking mark.

There was a nasty house fly in the room which kept landing on me, and the lighting was poor and I just couldn't find the thing to deal with it. My hunt went on for some time until I gave up. Victory was mine in the end though. I rose at 5am, and there was the fly, perched on a towel. With a downward swipe of my slipper, it was on its way to the floor at 50 knots where it spun for a couple of seconds before coming to rest on its back with its legs in the air. That particular fly would no longer be a source of irritation to anyone.

Road 40

From Road 40

Clouded sulphur butterfly on clover

4ᵗʰ August 2023   22154 – 22957

Rocky Mountain House to Hinton

18.144l = $27.20 at 22491 at Jasper

21.142l = $30.00 at 22956 at Hinton

I left Voyageur Motel early as the first glimmers of daybreak appeared. It was drizzling lightly, and I set off westwards joining the steady flow of traffic at 5:30am. I kept well back from the pickup in front of me and kept a sharp eye open for any wildlife that may be on the wide verge. I saw nothing, but was vigilant just in case. An elk through the window would be the finish of many things, and the little story would be over. After half an hour, I was able to relax more as the sky assumed a lighter grey and visibility improved.

After a couple of hours, I reached Saskatchewan River Crossing and turned right towards Jasper. Blue patches appeared in the sky and very quickly they spread and gave way to a glorious day However, in the mountains it was cold to start with. At Rocky Mountain House in the drizzle, it was 14C when I set off. Now just north of Saskatchewan River Crossing, it was 3C. As the sun rose, so did the warmth, soon reaching 23C. I was travelling over known ground on my way to Jasper, but was still impressed by the incredible mountain scenery, and stopped to top up my growing collection of photos.

It was too early for the officials to be in their little toll booths as I entered the national park. I had bought an annual pass, which I proudly hung on my internal mirror. This bit of coloured paper allowed me entry into all of Canada's national parks until August 2024. However, if you arrive at the kiosks before office hours, you're in anyway. Maybe rangers check your vehicle during the day; I don't know. The annual pass cost me $61.

I arrived at Jasper at 09:30, and filled with petrol, and then looked for the no through road to Lake Malign. This road is on the northeast of Jasper, and I had been told that it teemed with wildlife. I looked forward in anticipation to having to dodge bears, moose, caribou, elk, and such like. I saw no signs to Lake Malign from Jasper, so I followed the main highway north towards Edmonton. TomTom did not know of Lake Malign, so that resource was unhelpful on this occasion. I was reliant on the sheet map, where the Lake Malign turn looked a millimetre from Jasper! I thought I must have missed the turn, and was on the point of making a U-turn when the sign on the right to Malign Canyon appeared. It was not a sign to Lake Malign, but the Malign bit gave hope that this was the right turn. The Canadians are economical with directions. The only signs in great abundance, regularly repeated, are signs warning you of bears and all the other animals that we have previously mentioned.

I saw no animals on my way up the valley. I stopped for a walk by the river and saw what I believed to be elk pooh, and it was fresh. It was on a grassy flat by the water, and was the sort of place you could imagine the elk gathering for a drink and a chat, much the same as people congregate at a bar for the same purpose. There are conveniences near to a bar, but wildlife does not require these facilities. What needs to be done, gets done there and then; hence the material I had spotted on the ground. A couple nearby were pulling faces as they cleaned the said material from their son's shoes with a pointed stick. He had trodden in it. They had been on site during last night and informed me that the elk were there at 6am. I had missed them. Well, I guess that's par for the course.

I moved on to Malign Canyon, which is a deep depression with spectacular views across it. There were a number of people there admiring the view. They each had different explanations on the absence of bears. One said it was the wrong time of day. You needed to be around at dawn or dusk. Another said it was the wrong season. You needed to be there before June. I believe that to be wrong. Bears don't hibernate until the weather turns cold. In the lead up to the cold weather, they have to eat like mad to fatten up for the long sleep. The signs said it was berry season, and the bears would be busy right now. The lack of them tells me, and perhaps you, that they are in decline, and any that may be around want peace and quiet away from humans.

I continued up the valley to Medicine Lake, a large expanse of water, appearing salty round the margins, and areas that have drained, perhaps accounting for the name. People seem to like salty water as health giving when they are sick. People sit in such water for long periods to let it really get into the skin. They may drink the concentrated water as well. They call that "taking the water". There are places where you can do this sort of thing in the UK. They call them "spas". I tried to find out the role of this lake in the past, but the only thing the indigenous people are known to have been amazed by is the disappearance of this lake as if someone had pulled the plug out. This is apparently due to a very large underground cave system, which occasionally lets the lake in. Anyway, it's Medicine Lake and is occasionally a meeting place for bears, moose, and elk, but not today.

When you get to the lake, there is a layby where you are confronted by signs that point out a bald eagle's nest, high up on a snapped off dead tree. To avoid disturbance to the birds, the foreshore and the next layby, is closed off. Looking through my lens, I could see that the nest was deserted, and looked as if it had been for a long time. I made further enquiries, and found that the nest had not been used at all this year. The signs had been left there for effect.

I finally arrived at Lake Malign, but there were so many tourists that there were no parking places. The reserve car park for busy times was also full, and a lot were parked along the road, risking being towed away. I made my way slowly back down the valley. I was rewarded by elk at the roadside in two places. It was so wonderful to see them. The elk are magnificent animals with huge antlers. You'd think the antlers would have impeded their progress through the forest, but they seem to get by just fine. They certainly looked stunning. They tell you that these lovely animals attack people. I'm sure they could, but honestly, they appeared the most docile contented creatures out. If they had young with them, you might be more concerned, but all these elk wanted to do is eat grass and other herbs. I got some nice photos.

Then I proceeded to the junction with the Jasper to Edmonton highway, and turned right towards Hinton, where I had booked accommodation for the night as it was far cheaper than Jasper. I arrived at the Twin Pine Inn and Suite at 3:30pm. Here I checked in, and had a meal in the on-site restaurant. I asked the waiters if they knew any good locations for bear spotting. They said I needed to drive up road 40 to a place called Cadomin. There, it was teeming with bears, eagles and other wildlife. I took their advice, but found nothing apart from a lot of dust, and drove back to the main highway after a couple of hours of it, during which I covered 88km.

Then it happened. I was travelling down the main highway towards Hinton, and a bear crossed the road in front of me. I was travelling into the sun which was a pity as the bear just shows as a silhouette on the photos. Still, I was overjoyed to have seen the bear in the wild for the first time in my life. I've seen them in captivity in zoos, where many are in captivity, and that's a bit sad, but now, I'd seen one in its natural habitat. At the same time the point was illustrated, that it's no good going to look for these things. They are rare. You only see them by chance when they cross your path. Note also that the bear was not using the road as a corridor. It was crossing it. The reason it was crossing the road was to get to the other side. It's the old riddle, and once you've been caught with it a few times, you know the answer. This time it was a bear crossing the road, not a chicken. If you still want to catch people with this sort of riddle, you can ask, why did the toffee cross the road? The answer is, it was stuck to the chicken's foot.

Edith Lake

Medicine Lake

Lake Malign

Elk

Sawback range

5th August 2023   22957 – 23378

Hinton to McBride

14.75l = $26.83 at 23231 at Mt Robson

I left Hinton Twin Pine Suite at 6:30. The sky was absolutely clear, and it promised to be another glorious day. I went to check out, but there was nobody in reception. A faceless voice must have known I was about, for a voice called from another room, asking me to leave my key on the desk. The desire for face-to-face contact with the customer was not strong. I did as I was asked, and got under way.

I drove to Malign Lake again, hoping that getting there early would reveal more wildlife. Though early, it was already quite busy. In the UK, people tend to like what they call a "lie in". This concept seems unfamiliar to the Canadian who likes to be roaring around from first light onwards. Here they don't talk about the length of a journey in distance. They talk about the time it takes. In the UK we say that such and such a place is so many miles away. A Canadian will tell you how many hours it is away.

There was a group of people looking eagerly at the bald eagle's nest by Medicine Lake. Others were scanning the sky with binoculars, as instructed by the posters, which told tourists that if they weren't on the nest, the sky is where they would be seen. I stopped to advise them of the information I had, which is that the nest had not been used for over a year. The group walked away disgusted that they had been conned. A couple of local experts told me that I had burst their bubble. You see, this is the thing. Honesty is the best policy. Tell folk that the place is riddled with bears, and they will believe you because in the absence of personal experience, locals are expected to have the knowledge and to impart it to visitors. Once you find that you've been told nonsense, you never believe what you are told again, and that's a disadvantage. The truth isn't always what people want to hear but, at least, if you tell them the truth, they know where they are. If they want something else, they can always invent it in their own heads. So subtle is the human brain, that if you tell yourself something enough times, you will get to believe it. Politicians work on this principle. For example, when Covid came along, three men appeared. There were always three. Each stood behind a pulpit, and the message was that you had to stay home to save your life. This message was presented day after day and it was believed and the streets all went quiet. If they tried that tack again now, it wouldn't get the same response.

Anyway, I returned from the lake to a junction very close to the main Jasper to Edmonton Road, and turned left to Lake Anette. There was no wildlife visible, but the lake is lovely and well worth a visit. The water was very still and the reflection of the mountains was wonderful. The main peak visible from this lake is Pyramid Peak, which speaks for itself. It is an upward pointy mountain.

After absorbing the view and walking along the shore of the lake, I returned to the main road and turned left to Jasper. Jasper is quite a long town, especially when you travel through it at the imposed limit of 30kph. There were no horses, but the London to Holyhead horse drawn carriage went faster than that. They had to change the horses every now and then, and that's where stage inns came in. The horses would be given straw and provender, and the next set would take the coach onwards. Here in Jasper, you roll through the town being overtaken by the pigeons and pedal bikes. Once through the town, I joined the main highway again and travelled towards McBride.

Though still in the Rocky Mountains, which is a huge range stretching from Northern Canada down into the USA, the mountains were more spaced out and less dramatic than between Banff and Jasper. The highway led me up a pass between the Caribou Mountains on the left and the Rocky Mountains on the right. Both ranges were high and many were snow-capped. The road is called the "Yellowhead Pass". It isn't a mountain pass in the UK sense of the word. There are no hairpin bends and steep gradients. You just drive up, along with the trucks. It is a gradual thing. There are some overtaking stretches, and down the other side of Canadian passes, there are signs telling you to get into low gear, and there are runaway lanes where you can escape and lose all your pent-up speed on a ramp, if your brakes fail. The road follows rivers, the main one being Fraser River.

Once I left Jasper National Park, I came to the next time zone. There are six time zones across Canada, indicating its huge size. In some ways, it's small because you can cross it in a few days. It would take longer to walk though, and you'd need two or three pairs of shoes. At the time zone, my sat nav went back another hour and shortly afterwards, the phone followed suit.

I came to Mount Robson, an outstanding snow-capped peak with a trail going up to a couple of lakes. A black bear cub ran across the road, but was too quick for a photo. The mountain and river views were wonderful. I stayed there for an hour to take it all in.

Then I drove on to McBride where I had booked accommodation at the Travelodge. I checked in and then went into town to look at the railway history. Towns like this were well served with passenger trains, but they fell into disuse when the private car came along, and the stations were closed. McBride seemed a nice little town that had been let run down. There was no pub; it had closed down. The station had become the community centre of the town, and had a nice café where coffee and cake were served with a smile. You pay for the first coffee, but subsequent fill-ups are free. Elderly folk outside engaged in conversation. I explained that I was looking for bears. One man said that he used to go hunting them thirty years ago at Dunster, a nearby village. He used a bow and arrow. He said that regularly there were seventeen bears there. Now you see none. There were also lots of moose. Unfortunately, they are reckoned to be good to eat. Hunting brings fun to those warped enough to get enjoyment out of it, but it brings down the numbers. Hunting is one of many pressures that takes its toll on wildlife. Canada has amazing wildlife, but if it wants to preserve it, in the words of many school reports, it could do better if it tried. There are massive efforts designed to stop human interaction with wildlife, and to stop all feeding. Fine, but feeding is probably less harmful than bullets and forest fires. We have to take a holistic approach to wildlife care. Mostly, humans are in competition with wildlife. Competition is normally for habitat, and as the human population soars, wildlife declines because its native range is reduced and turned to concrete, or manicured in park settings.

Black bear

Elk

6th August 2023   23378 – 23737

McBride to Blue River and back to McBride

25.583l = $45.00 at 23737 at McBride

A continental breakfast was included in my room hire at Travelodge. After that, I drove down some back grit lanes and found a quiet spot to worship, appreciating the wonderful things I had been able to enjoy.

Then I continued down the lanes to Dunster, a tiny village that was a thriving community in the early 1900s. Now, its railway station is a museum. The railway line still sees freight and occasional passenger trains, but they pass through rather than stop. Dunster has a little general store that does nearly everything, and keeps the village going. A huge vote of thanks is given by the locals for the way this little store kept going and served the community during Covid. Their thanks are recorded on the store front. Covid brought great hardship to many because normal movement was banned. Not only did this restrict availability of necessities; it restricted contact between people and there was huge psychological damage as a result. We are a communal animal. Distancing ourselves from one another doesn't do any good. Most live with one or more people, but when circumstances bring loneliness, a community hub, and folks to chat with, is as vital as any prescription medicine. Isolation might stop us catching a cold, but mental issues from loneliness was underestimated, and even ignored. Anyway, the little village of Dunster with its handful of houses, has kept going, and the vital link is its little store. Trains roll past on the south, and vehicles roar past on the main highway a few miles to the north. Little Dunster sits in the middle on its grit lane like a time capsule in a mad world. Beautiful views of the Rockies to the north and Caribou mountains to the south make this a delightful spot.

I continued down grit roads which were quiet, peaceful, and dusty. The railway is much straighter, and I crossed it several times. There aren't barriers out here in the wilds. There are flashing lights and the requirement to stop, look and listen. Trains always sound their horns when approaching the crossings, and you would have to be very hard of hearing not to detect it. The horns have a minimum output of 143dB at one metre, but even at one hundred metres, they are uncomfortably loud, which is what they are meant to be. Accidents on level crossings in Canada are rare, whereas in the UK there are about fifty every week. Drivers in the UK can mostly communicate at a basic level, and would know that if they were hit by a train, they come off worse. However, a lot of drivers persist in pulling out in front of things, and that includes trains. When they pull out in front of other cars, the inconvenienced driver will usually avert a tragedy by taking avoiding action. This is less easy for a train weighing hundreds of tons. In Canada, trains don't weigh a few hundred tons; they weigh thousands of tons. Anyway, my Nissan Versa is no match for ten thousand tons of Canadian Pacific rolling stock, carrying possibly twenty thousand tons of coal. I tend to stop and have a jolly good look up and down the line before crossing. You never know, it might have a dodgy horn, and the crossing lights might not be working. Some of the crossings don't even have lights. They rely on people being sensible. Try that where I came from!

I followed the dirt road until coming to a T junction near Valemount, on the highway south towards Blue River. At this point, I'd like to tell you about Canadian roads. The bulk of them have a nice smooth surface made of concrete, or more commonly now, from asphalt. They are still laying smooth surfaces which are almost infinitely better than the ballast strewn roads in the UK, Australia, and New Zealand. Unfortunately, the Canadians have got to hear about the UK cheap method of road surfacing, and they have now spent six million dollars in trying it out on Highway 16. I guess it will become more prevalent in time as a cost saving measure. For the moment, I cherish the smooth quiet motoring of Canadian roads. I tried to have an intelligent interchange of letters with the UK Highways agency on this subject, but sadly, they weren't at that level of mental capability, and they revealed this in their replies. They believe that the ballast strewn road is quieter than a smooth surface by 2.5dB. I have access to a calibrated dB monitor which reveals the opposite. To the human ear, a smooth surface generates much less tyre noise, but you can argue with that feeling. You can't argue with a calibrated instrument, whose accuracy is traceable right back to the National Physics Laboratory. You can tell which is the quietest by driving on it, but the monitor provides the actual data. The ballast strewn surface gives more noise and friction, resulting in poorer fuel economy, and more tyre wear. There is nothing to recommend the rough surface apart from it's cheaper than laying the surface properly.

At Blue River, there is a river safari, where for $120, they take you up the Fraser River to look for wildlife. There are meant to be bald eagles soaring overhead, moose and black bear by the river side, and a few other species that you may or may not see. In the event, I saw no wildlife apart from a heron, and a few small birds. It was a lovely trip. First, they take you on a battery powered twin hulled canoe, which they convey you to a mooring point in the centre of a lake. There you transfer to a jet boat which takes you a few miles further upstream. The river is shallow and the jet boat is the only way of getting further. We roared along at 50kph (30mph) on this craft which planes over the water rather than sitting in it. The only bit of the boat actually in the water is the prop. Everything else is flying. I would have thought all the noise and confusion would have driven the wildlife away, but the staff said no, the animals had got used to the boats, and were content with it.

The complete lack of wildlife was explained away. Whichever bedtime story you accept, there was a lovely boat ride, but devoid of wildlife. One story is that the bears had eaten their cubs. Another is that a pack of wolves had just passed through and eaten everything, apart from a small remnant that had moved away. The way you can ensure the presence of wildlife on these occasions, is to feed it. That's illegal, and one safari company has just been fined $35,000 for doing it. The bears came to the feeding post, and were happy. The visitors were happy. The company was happy. Presumably, those in receipt of the fine were happy. As we can see, it's an ill-wind that blows nobody any good.

Back on Terra Firma, I had a quick coffee, and set off for my second night at McBride Travelodge, arriving at 6:30pm, in time for a bowl of soup and a pint at nearby Sandman Inn.

Dunster store

Grit road to Valemouth

The only black bear of the day

Heading up the Fraser River

7ᵗʰ August 2023   23737 – 24308

Mc Bride to Houston

12.202l = $20.00 at 23956 at Prince George

16.676l = $30.00 at 24292 at Houston

I had a fairly long drive today, so I left the Travelodge at McBride at 5:30. The sky was mainly blue, but as I looked back, there was a fantastic golden sunrise, so I stopped to photograph it. The journey west was peaceful to begin with, but it grew increasingly busy as time continued. I had left the highest mountains now, but distant views of snowy peaks were visible for most of the journey. A blueish tinge to the atmosphere was the first sign of forest fires that I had seen. I had heard that the fires were at a critical stage in British Columbia with a lot of fires out of control. Rain was expected for the next two days, but this was not thought sufficient to extinguish the fires.

Keeping to the speed limits meant that as usual, I was one of the slowest vehicles on the road, and, I do not like frustrated cars behind me. Overtaking was often hazardous, as lanes for this purpose were only provided for short distances every 13km or so. I kept pulling over to let the speeders past, which shouldn't have been necessary as I was doing a few kph over the limit. It is clear that the general view is that the police turn a blind eye to moderate speeding, believing that no action will be taken unless they are doing more than 20kph over the limit. In theory, anything over the limit is an offence. There are a number of senior politicians in the UK who want all tolerance to be removed and fines always dished out for only 1mph over the limit. While these people clearly have vindictive streaks and mind problems, tearing along at 20kph over the limit is obviously deliberate contempt for the rules, and should not be allowed. I can think of circumstances when very high speed would be sensible, if not legal, but to do it all the time is plainly wrong, and that's what most drivers here do. There are two possible reasons for this. Either the speed limits are far too low, or, the enforcement needs tightening up with penalties and detection rates that discourage this behaviour. It's a whole different ethos than that of the UK where the norm is to drive at significantly less than the limit, and it is considered socially acceptable to drive like this, and is actively encouraged. In Canada, many journeys are long, and the drivers like to accomplish their mission in good time. This contrasts with the UK where the length of journeys tends to be shorter and drivers have little concern for the time they take.

The speed limit today was up and down like a yoyo, and repeat signs were not regular, so often, I did not know what the limit was. The limit on Highway 16 is 90kph or 100kph, but a wide range of other limits were imposed for different things. I saw 20, 30, 40, 50, 60, 70, and 80 limits today. I thought the 20kph limit in one town was really silly, but there it was. Constant vigilance was required to spot and comply with all this variation.

In addition to concentrating on the speed limit signs, and my speedometer, I was asked by dozens of signs to be aware that I was on a wildlife corridor, the suggestion being that the road was teeming with large animals. Pictures of them were displayed. I was meant to keep a close watch on the verge in case these creatures leapt out in front. I did have a great thrill when I reached Fraser Lake. A black bear crossed the main highway. It was clear that the bear is not an aggressive animal. Sensing human activity with the opening of the car door, the bear put a spurt on and ran into the undergrowth. I got a couple of photos, and was overjoyed to have had three bear sightings during my trip.

Prince George appeared to be very run down. Even on the main road through there was a large area given over to a shanty town made up of tents and other materials. People of no fixed abode, and some from the flats above, were huddled in various places. This is sad, and though Prince George does not have the record for homelessness in Canada, it does have a sizeable problem.

I arrived at Houston, but initially had problems finding "Pleasant Valley Motel" where I had booked accommodation for the night. Again, the address in the TomTom was incorrect, and I asked locals for guidance. It was on the main E16 road further than TomTom's ideas. I checked in, and then went out to seek a meal. All the outlets I found were of the fast-food variety. There are a few exceptions, but mostly, the offering is protein and carbohydrates, not vegetables.

I watched a freight train pass through Houston. The first 115 trucks were filled with coal. These trucks are 30 tons each and have capacity for 100 tons of coal. There were an additional 52 trucks of a closed type, and I had no idea of what might be in them. Even if they were empty, I worked out that the train weighed nearly 20,000 tons. Railways are certainly a good way of shifting bulk freight. You could argue about the use of coal. Canada has signed up to net zero carbon initiatives, but it appears that mining coal for China doesn't count provided it's not burned at home! The UK shut all its coal mines some years ago, sealing the potential energy underground. Were that coal to be tapped, it is enough to power the UK for about 200 years. When our mines were shut down, it made a negligible difference to global pollution, because other countries like China and India supported by the vast coal mining activities of Canada, USA, and Australia, were burning it at an almost unimaginable rate.

Canada can talk about carbon footprints when the nations meet to discuss these matters, but while they are sending huge amounts of the coal to Asia, and burning millions of acres of forest every year, the talks seem rather meaningless. We realise that what drives the real world is energy and money. Cutting back on pollution is talked about in different rooms to those where coal and energy deals are made. In the UK, we had some large coal fired power stations, including one local to me in Shropshire. The Ironbridge power station burned about 67,000 tons of coal per week and made lots of electricity. Other coal power stations shut down were much bigger. That's all very good, but where does the electricity come from. There is nuclear power that many fawn after, but all the countries using it have had their disasters, and all produce awfully toxic nuclear waste that lasts for centuries. We had Windscale. America had Three Mile Island. Ukraine had Chernobyl.

Japan had Fukushima. We've had to close another nuclear power station down due to cracks in its structure. Nuclear Power is unsafe because it occasionally goes wrong, and when it does, the whole world is threatened, not just from the initial contamination, but for decades afterwards. The UK completed its national grid in 1935 and we all got dependent on electricity in our homes. We made it from coal and were easily able to provide enough for our needs then. The population was a fraction of what it is now, and use of electricity was much less. Now, most domestic and industrial equipment works on electricity, and we even want cars to run on it. The government made a big push for electric cars, telling everyone that the sale of new cars would only be electric after 2030. They didn't do their homework before passing the edict. There isn't enough electricity to go round now and we have to wire a lot of it over from France. France provides not megawatts, or gigawatts, but terawatts into our electricity grid. How will we cope when over 30 million electric cars need charging? So, the date has been pushed back. The hope of countries to get away from burning fuel and becoming self-sufficient in renewable energy is a quantum leap from our current situation, and one that is unlikely to be bridged any time soon.

McBride sunrise

Purden Lake

West from Six Mile Summit

8ᵗʰ August 2023   24308 – 24737

Houston to Prince Rupert

I left Pleasant Valley motel, Houston at 07:00, and the journey to Prince Rupert was a modest 258 miles. I drove into increasingly wet and murky weather.

The road had signs every few miles warning moose and elk, but none of these animals were around this morning. I passed through a number of villages and towns. In between were massive fields devoted to silage production. There were thousands of bales of it, presumably ready for the winter when this area would be under feet of snow, and all the cattle would have to be kept inside.

Despite it being said that Canada was having a hot dry summer, the rivers were mostly in spate and waterfalls were spectacular. This was mainly due to melting glaciers rather than rainfall. The flow was so high that the salmon were finding difficulty in progressing upstream. Salmon are migratory, spending years at sea, but coming back to the stream of their birth when it is time for them to spawn. Nobody understands what triggers the migration of many different species. The time comes, and off they go. The salmon crossing the oceans and finding the very stream they hatched in, is something of a miracle. It's all designed to make us think, and marvel at the complexity and wonder of the Creation. Creatures are created, and though not having the power of reason per se, they have abilities that outmatch ours in different ways.

I came to a little town called Witset. Here the Buckly River has a waterfall. The salmon were trying to leap up the fall and progress to their spawning place. I was disturbed to see a group of people who had constructed aluminium ladders across the falls, and were trying to catch the salmon in nets. It seemed rotten to me to wait until they arrived from the ocean having done perhaps more than a thousand miles, only to be pulled out with a net. I made my feelings known, but it was explained that the fish were different kinds of salmon, and the purpose of the catch was to carry out research. The fish were weighed and tagged and allowed to continue their journey. There is concern at their depletion. Of course, "climate change" is dished out as the reason for all natural ills, but salmon are caught in their millions, with insufficient regard for sustainable fishing. Extinction of many species is down to human greed, and it is true to say that humans have done more damage to this planet than any other creature. We think we know best, but history shows a different story which repeats itself as we fail to learn. People study different branches of nature and go down a narrow route of study in great depth. They become experts in that narrow field, but frequently don't see the relationship this has with the rest of the world. They think up schemes to enhance the wellbeing of the species of their interest, and expect nature to comply with their ideas. Sometimes, it's better to care for the environment by not interfering with it.

When I was a boy, the global population was 2.5 billion. Though this was a lot of people, the natural world was not overwhelmed, and current fishing and harvesting practices could cope. As the human population has rocketed, so has creature capture, and in many cases, this is not sustainable. When I was at school, I was taught that by the year 2000, the population would be 5 billion and the world would be unable to support this, and there would be mass famine. Now the population is heading for 8 billion, and the food supply is stretched in many places. In the UK, we were self-sufficient in food. Yes, we did import tea and coffee and other non-essential items, but basic foods were mostly British. Stuff that was out of season like fruit, was preserved so that we could still eat it in the winter. Now, we don't grow half our food, and are reliant on other countries selling it to us, and transporting it from thousands of miles away. As we convert more of our land to concrete and our population continues to spiral upwards, how long will the supermarket shelves be able to satisfy our needs? Ransacking the earth's finite resources is not a long-term solution to meeting our needs. It can only go on so long. People who are worried about wild salmon numbers get upset and try to set fishing quotas and moderate catches. Although this is helpful, some nations refuse to comply, and the destruction continues. We have quite a lot of knowledge and ability, but do we have wisdom? Wisdom is the ability to put knowledge into profitable use. If we are honest, we have to say that this is often lacking. Anyway, I was relieved that the Kinset salmon catch was not commercial. I hoped all their fridges would not to be full of salmon that night though!

I stopped many times to take photos and try to get a feel for the real Canada. I eventually arrived at Prince Rupert at 2pm. I had booked accommodation at The Pacific Inn for two nights. My room was nice, and it was great to have free carparking underneath the building where the car stayed cool and dry. Poor sound insulation was the same here as many places. It was possible to shut the doors noisily, and some people were exceedingly good at it. Some were slamming their doors with a force that shook the walls and rattled the windows. They like to ensure the doors are fastened here. I set off round town, the main purpose being to get food items from Safeway, the cheapest supermarket chain I have found in Canada so far. I found the Prince Rupert fire department on my walk, a portion of which had been turned into a museum for the fire and police departments. A retired volunteer was on duty and he welcomed me in, and took me on a guided tour. His knowledge was great, having worked for 35 years in that department. It was a most interesting visit. He gave me a reproduction fire department badge as a souvenir, that I will always treasure. We discussed the wildfires, now out of control, because they were monitored rather than extinguished in their early stages. They are now the worst that Canada has ever known. It is inexcusable that some of these fires are started by careless discarding of cigarettes. The forests need dead wood clearing out. Dead trees are ready to burn fiercely and should not be left there in large numbers. There should be firebreaks to slow the spread of fire and give easy access to sections of forestry. There are none currently. In British Columbia where the fires are so devastating, there are hundreds of miles of dense forest without a break.

I had another pleasant surprise in Prince Rupert. 1 bought postage stamps from a supermarket for $1 each (59p). I asked if they were suitable for mail to the UK. Yes, was the answer. I said that stamps for sending mail between towns in the UK was 75p. I asked the shop keeper again, and he assured me that the $1 stamps would be fine as it turned out to be. My letters and cards all reached their destination. It seemed incongruous that internal mail in the UK costs 75p per item, but I can post in Canada, and it has to cross Canada, and the Atlantic, and the UK, and all that costs 59p! I was sure something was not right. Indeed, it turned out to be the case that stamps to the UK cost $2.75 each, but all my mail arrived safely, and I thank Canada Post for that.

I had my evening meal in The Pacific Inn. The meal was good, and included broccoli and carrots, which I hadn't seen for some time. I asked for a real ale, a term that the waiters didn't understand. They only had lagers, and a locally produced beer in a can was $14, so I had orange juice instead. The meal was probably the nicest I've had in Canada so far, and was $38 (£22.75) including the expected 15% tip. I guess it's not too far beyond UK prices, depending where you go.

My room, in common with nearly all Canadian motels, did not have a kettle. They have a coffee maker with a tiny hotplate that takes between half an hour and an hour to boil and make coffee. I gave up and had water instead. I figured that bears, moose, and elk drink water and they are strong enough!

Mountains at Evelyn

Salmon research at Witset

Pacific Inn at Prince Rupert

9ᵗʰ August 2023   24737 – 24795

At Prince Rupert

25.45l = $45.79 at 24746 at Prince Rupert

I had tried online to book a ferry from Prince Rupert to Port Hardy at the north of Vancouver Island. As with many British Columbia (BC) ferries, all dates for the days ahead were fully booked. I completed an online waiting list form, but received no reply. I decided to present myself at the BC ferry terminal and ask in person for a sea passage. The alternative was to retrace my steps eastwards and reach Vancouver Island from the south, or omit it altogether. A possible alternative would have been exploration of the far north of Canada. This would have disobeyed the limits of my hire car range. Car hire is not as simple as paying for the days you hire it at a fixed rate. There are one-way fees, insurances, deposits that took the hire fee to about £3500. Seeing that a new Nissan Versa costs around £16,000, the car would have paid for itself in a few months. I believe that the profit margins on these hire firms is large, and a little expedition to the Yukon would not have been a major issue, unless I had needed to be retrieved from there, in which case, I guess the total bill would have been on me. I entered the ferry terminal into my TomTom and drove there, but the TomTom interpretation was wrong. I ended up at the opposite end of the city to the BC Ferry Terminal, and as it was early, everything was shut. I spotted an employee letting himself into one of the dock buildings, and I asked him for directions, which he gave helpfully and clearly.

I was glad of the unnecessary detour to the wrong end of the city for one reason. On some railings by the dock was perched a large bald-headed eagle. Here again was showed the principle of wildlife spotting in Canada. You are largely wasting your time going on safaris and places where they tell you the wildlife is. Those are simply a well-oiled tourist machine. Instead, you see wildlife when you aren't looking for it. Animals cross the main highway in front of you, or perch on things in front of you. They surprise you with their close proximity, but when you turn up with a company of fifteen or twenty others, led by a guide, these self-conscious and shy creatures slip away before you've spotted them. I had scanned the skies and looked through lenses into empty nests, all to no avail, but here, a few feet away was the bald-eagle, looking straight at me. I took a few photos.

Then I drove to the other end of the city and found the BC Ferry Terminal, and waited in a queue to speak to an officer. When my turn came, she tried to book me onto a ferry, but her computer would not allow her to proceed. It was a common case of human tries to say yes, but computer says no. People talk in hushed voices about AI, which stands for Artificial Intelligence. They have read too many science fiction stories, and believe that computers will take over the world and displace us from our positions. The truth is that computers can't do anything unless humans have programmed them to. The worry is not computers doing their own thing, but humans that have programmed dangerous decisions into them. Computers are good at processing huge amounts of data. Humans aren't, and it takes a long time for a person to collate data. However, the decision made upon analysing the data is not generally left to a computer. For example, computers analyse our skies and gather data on every machine up there, but any response is made by humans. Microchips will only do what we've programmed them to do. They don't have any innate intelligence, or emotional feelings. Anyway, the officer asked me to stand to one side while she ticketed the other customers in the queue behind me. After half an hour she tried again, and though her system would not allow booking, she allocated me a reservation, and said that if I presented myself at the terminal at 5:30am in two days, there was a good chance that I would be accommodated.

I returned to The Pacific Inn and extended my booking by another night. Next, I decided to visit the Cannery, now a museum, but formerly a salmon fishing and canning venture that made fortunes in the early 1900s. It's situated at Port Edward, just a few miles away. On arrival, I paid the senior entrance fee of only $12. This was when I realised how old I must look. Well-meaning folk say I don't look my age, but the officer at the Cannery entrance offered me a senior ticket before I asked. That wouldn't have happened if there was a chance that I could have been below the concession age. A guided tour was about to commence, so I had arrived just in time. The tour was fascinating. The Cannery was set up by entrepreneurs who had turned up to take part in the gold rush that was at its height. Gold made a fortune for some, but huge disappointments and strife attended the consuming lust for wealth. Gold has brought joy and sadness in a ratio that is hard to be exact about. Suffice it to say that gold is avidly sought, but does not always bring lasting joy to those who acquire it. A canny chap spotted salmon leaping up the river in large numbers and decided that here was a more certain way of making money. Prince Rupert is remote from the rest of the world. You can't transport fresh fish to Vancouver and across the world, because by the time it arrives, it's very smelly. Really smelly fish, unless you are a seagull, is not very appetising. Hence, the canning process was born. Initially everything was done by hand, using the large readily available manpower. The social side of the employees is interesting. There were Chinese, Japanese, and indigenous people, now called "First Nation". These groups would have nothing to do with each other, and each group was given its own tasks, and accommodated in separate blocks. The houses were very basic, and yet, had many artefacts that I remember from childhood. My early childhood was very primitive compared with today, and my facilities were very similar in many ways to the houses on the cannery site. Only the management had more luxury.

The second world war brought America and Canada in when the Japanese took it into their heads to gain victory over the whole world, and made a start by bombing Pearl Harbour. Until that event, America had supported the Allies with equipment to help against the German attempt on world domination, but now, they were very much in it. At home, this entailed the internment of all Japanese, and this included the cannery workers. This imposed a labour shortage at the cannery, and this is where mechanisation began.

The fish were being hauled out of the Skeena River and estuary in ever increasing numbers as the mechanical lines were able to process faster than by hand. The cotton nets were replaced by stronger, and longer lasting nylon, and the cannery grew to a huge organisation. Nobody gave a thought as to its sustainability. They don't now, and in those days, limiting fish catches was not considered until stocks were severely depleted. The thing with us is we tend to notice when our cupboards aren't full, but at work, we tend to use stuff without thinking about the long-term consequences. How many times will we pillage the earth's resources without thinking about them running out? Today, overfishing is still a major problem, but in many places, salmon farming has replaced wild salmon fishing. The cannery stopped canning in 1968. The only thing that continued was a process called reduction to make fishmeal, but in 1981, it closed and fell into disuse. It was handed over to the town in 1987, and what hadn't been sold off, was preserved and now, it is a very interesting museum.

There were only a few people on the cannery tour, and we got to know each other. The final part was watching a film of the whole history of the site. I had seen a couple looking at me during the film, and eventually the lady came across and said, "would you mind if we asked a big favour from you?". They had been ripped off by a taxi, that had charged them $81 for the short ride one way from Prince Rupert to Port Edward, and wondered if I could give them a lift back to town. I was only too happy to oblige. The couple were good company, and I was going back anyway. There were approaching their golden wedding anniversary, and were doing a few trips in their celebratory year. They treated me to a nice lunch in The Pavillion Restaurant when we arrived back in Prince Rupert. Here, we exchanged details in order to stay in touch. They are Bob and Joan. They were farmers from Missouri, and invited me to stay with them if I visited the States, which I had already been thinking of.

After leaving them, I visited the Wheelhouse Brewery. Whyever its products are not on tap in local restaurants, is beyond me. For the first time since my arrival in Canada, I had a real ale on tap, a live beer, a medicinally excellent product, full of natural goodness. This comes in sharp contrast with the zany sugar solutions desired by most people. I thought that with its aid, I may be able to see all the whales that were said on notices, to frequent the harbour entrance. Of course, there were none. I did see salmon leaping as they left the Pacific Ocean, and started their last few hundred miles up the Skeena River. I imagined they were leaping for joy. A local chap said they were doing it to clean their gills. This disappointed me somewhat, but I don't know if his information is right. Until I have it from a trustworthy source, the salmon were happy. My goldfish don't leap like this!

I walked back to my accommodation, stopping at the Wallmart Store on the way back. This was my first Wallmart experience ever. Here, I met pleasant staff, who asked if they could help me. This was a novel and nice touch. I was amazed at the bewildering display of everything from food to furniture, all at affordable prices. I spotted chocolate at half the price I had seen anywhere else, and invested in a couple of bars.

Bald eagle

North Pacific Cannery

Mechanisation at the cannery

Bob and Joan

10th August 2023   24795 – 24818

At Prince Rupert

Today was infill between my time planned in Prince Rupert, and my hoped-for ferry trip to Port Hardy. Bob and Joan had asked if we could spend the day together, going on one of the local trails. I readily complied. They chose the Butze Rapids Trail, with a start time of 10am. I picked my new friends up from their accommodation and drove to the trailhead.

We set off in fine weather though heavy clouds risked precipitation later. I had been warned by a guide that this trail was frequented by bears and wolfs, and he said that I should make a lot of noise while I was walking round, in order to warn these abundant creatures away. We badly wanted to see these creatures, so we crept round very quietly to avoid frightening them away. Perhaps we should have done a lot of heavy clumping instead. We saw none. However, we did get a fine surprise when a large owl flew out of a tree and settled in another one a short distance away. We slowly walked up to the new perching point and got some nice photos. I later identified the owl as a barred owl.

Apart from not seeing the larger wildlife, the walk was lined with lots of plants; some of which had been helpfully labelled. This was an area of tropical rainforest, which seemed incorrectly named, as it was much cooler here that places more commonly recognised as tropical, like northeast Australia. Anyway, there we are. The plants were typical of rainforest, including many air plants that hug from the trees. One of the predominant ground plants with huge leaves was called skunk cabbage. I would have expected a revolting smell from a plant of this name. Yet, crushed leaves and flower heads had no detectable odour. Looking it up afterwards indicates that this plant is slightly narcotic, and named after that property. The trees were mainly coniferous and varied in size. The largest were real giants and were a kind of cedar. Below them grew shrubs including blueberries. Since there were plenty of berries, and they are staple food of bears at this time of year, led to the conclusion that there were no bears in this area. If there were, why had they left the berries for us to find and eat.

The walk opened onto a plain grassy area across which you could imagine elk roaming, but all was very quiet. Eventually we descended to the Skeena River, where we had beautiful views of the river across to the hills beyond. Here you could imagine moose paddling about in the shallows, but again, there was nothing in the wildlife stakes. The river at this point is a huge lake, but we continued downstream to a point where it narrows and gives rise to the rapids which change direction with the tides, to either fill the lake on the incoming tide, or empty it on the outgoing tide. We arrived when the tide was fully out, and the rapids were not flowing appreciably.

We completed the circular walk in three hours, allowing time to sample the Tall Trees Trail nearby. This trail is named after the very tall trees that are a prominent feature of the walk. Drawn up towards the light, they are giants, and some are also of large girth as well as height. We followed the trail for about 1km, but when rain started, we called it a day and returned to the car, and from there back to Prince Rupert where Bob and Joan treated me to another nice lunch, this time at the Wheelhouse Brewery.

We finished the day in the city museum, which took us through the history of the area, showing the heritage of the indigenous people, the industry, and way of life. This went on to include the early white settlers. It ended up in the inevitable gift shop.

I then returned to The Pacific Inn, and packed, and retired early so that I could get down to the ferry terminal by 5am.

Barred owl   *Butze Rapids trail*

11ᵗʰ August 2023   24818 – 24821

Prince Rupert to Port Hardy

I had been told that provided I showed up at the vehicle lane entry at 5:30am, there would be a good chance that I could sail to Port Hardy at the north of Vancouver Island. It's an all-day trip of 523km (314 miles). Never one to be late, I set my alarm for 4am, and had an early but sleepless night. Just prior to 4am, I went into a deep sleep, and woke with a start when the alarm went off. It's always the way. I had already packed, so all I had to do was check out of The Pacific Inn and drive to the terminal. I arrived before the staff, at 4:45am. It was raining steadily and purposefully, and it looked like the inadequate Canadian forestry firefighting service had its wish. A few inches of rain are a blow to any fire, and far more successful than a few bushwhackers with their safety sticks. Everything was saturated, and the day had that sort of greyness that persists for days on end in the UK. The sooty firefighters would be heaving a sigh of relief.

The vehicle entry gate was opened at 5am, and as I was first in the queue, I moved forward to speak to the operative. I showed him my reservation document. He directed me to Lane 9, which I later found out was the hopeful's lane, reserved for those who would be allowed to board if there was space after everyone else was fitted in. I then went into the terminal where I was told to sit down until I was called. There were only three hopeful's. Another turned up on a motorcycle, and he was accommodated straight away because a bike can fit in anywhere really. There were six who had gone on the waiting list, but only three of us turned up. In the event we were all accommodated. The fare for the ride is $642.90, which is not bad considering the distance, and the long journey by road to get down to Vancouver and then the shorter crossing to Nanaimo. I don't think ride is the correct term for travel by boat, but it should be. We ride a bike, car, train, and horse. We even ride the waves, but we sail a boat. The thing is that boats don't have sails these days. They have a few flags fluttering in the breeze, but it's unlikely that these have any effect on the forward motion. It's all done by a propeller which is like an aeroplane, except that the propeller draws water past the boat whereas the aeroplane propeller draws air past the plane. Now here's a funny thing. You don't ride in an aeroplane either. You fly in a plane, but, if you stand outside the plane on its wing, then you do ride the plane. However, most people prefer to sit inside.

The boat was the "Northern Explorer", and was a large seven deck tub. There is another layer higher up, but that is reserved for the mariners. There are ropes across the stairs to stop you venturing up there. I paid an extra $40 for a seat in the "Aurora Lounge" which sits over the bridge. The bridge is the peculiarly named bit where the captain sits with his navigation aids. I don't know if he still has a wheel to twiddle, or if it's all done electronically these days. I prefer knobs and wheels as you feel more connected with the business than touch screens that you hope work, but sometimes fail. The Aurora Lounge give a bird's eye view ahead whereas if you sit at the side of the boat or the back (called the stern for some reason), you can only see half the story.

I had hoped to see whales on this trip, and had checked with a couple who had travelled the opposite direction the day before. They had seen seven whales, of which two were orcas, and the rest were humpbacks. My first task once on board was to get breakfast, and this was quite nice. It rained for the whole 16-hour trip. The only thing that varied was the rate at which it came down. Visibility was also poor. There were a few whale sightings and I managed to video a pair of humpbacks in the distance. They didn't exactly blow raspberries at the boat, but they ejected fountains of water upwards, and then dived and disappeared. I liked the way they did this. The tails were the last thing to slip below the surface, making a sort of gesture at the boat as they did so. It thrilled me to see these majestic creatures for the first time in my life. I have seen two orcas before in northern Scotland, but no other whales. I had someone excitedly pointing out whales in New Zealand once, but they turned out to be patches of seaweed.

We stopped at Bella Bella on the route to drop off some passengers and take more on. Bella Bella isn't a duplicated word. It really is what this place is called. I guess we all have places of significance in our lives that we would like to duplicate, but it gets tedious when the name has three of four syllables, so we usually only say it once per sentence, but here it's Bella Bella. We were there longer than expected, and still had six hours to go. Some of the remaining journey was on more open Pacific, and it wasn't rough, but there was a good swell that made this large boat roll gently from side to side. I prefer a smooth ride, but the sea is prone to be uneven in places. Anyway, we eventually moored up at Port Hardy at 00:30. I tried a few hotels and motels close to the dock, but all were full. There was no WiFi to log onto on the boat or now. I tried a filling station for advice, and was told to try the Pioneer Motel. By this time, it was 01:30, so I stayed in the car until dawn.

BC Ferry to Port Hardy

Murky weather on-route

12th August 2023   24821 – 25031

At Port Hardy

15.08.21 = $30.00 at 24865 at Port Hardy

At 6am, I stretched my uncomfortable body, shook myself, and drove to the Pioneer Motel, just outside Port Hardy. It lacked the glamour of the Port Hardy Hotels by the ferry terminal, but it was quiet, friendly, much more reasonably priced, and had accommodation available. I was told by someone that the reason for the low price was that it was the worst place. Well let me tell you that it was fine, and far better than nights in the car. Here's the thing. Most people don't have small cars, although they used to. They have things the size of living rooms now, and I'm sure that you can stretch yourself out flat in the back of them in a sleeping bag, and be comfortable. A small car is often called a sedan, which was the name for a chair for carrying one person, while it was carried on long sticks by two porters. The occupant usually felt very important. The car has come a long way since then, but it's still a few chairs fixed in a shaped box. With a little ingenuity, it could be transformed into a couple of beds, but they haven't gone down that route, and therefore, it's jolly uncomfortable to sleep in. I was thankful for the Pioneer Motel and booked a couple of nights there.

Then I set off for Coal Harbour and Cape Scott. I had heard that the northwest coast of Vancouver Island was very nice, and I could pick out a minor road there on my map, and I decided to try it. The quality of the road was dire and it was very dirty and exceedingly rough. I kept at it for a couple of hours and had made little progress. I decided that discretion was the better part of valour and packed it in, and headed back towards Port Hardy. I had only just turned round when a strange light came on the dashboard and a message asking me to check the tyre pressure. This was a worry as I was a long way in time from anywhere. I knew I had a skinny wheel in the boot, but it wasn't up to the terrain I was on. I just hoped I could make it back to town. The Vice Versa wasn't that helpful. It just kept telling me to check the tyre pressure. It didn't tell me which tyre. It must have known the tyre to report the problem. A diagram of the four corners of the car with a red dot indicating the faulty tyre would be useful, but the Vice Versa doesn't go that far. If I go to the doctor and let him know that I have a pain, he's going to ask where. If I tell him that he'll have to find that out, he's probably going to send me away. I got out of the car and checked the wheels and it was the rear offside tyre that was soft. I felt all round the tyre and could see, feel or hear any abnormality or air loss. It was evidently a slow puncture. I made my way slowly back to Port Hardy and stopped at the Coop Garage. Here I asked for compressed air. There was a line which was free to use, but there was no pressure gauge. I put some air in, but was not sure how much I needed. I moved on to the next garage. This one had a compressed air line which costs

$1 to use, but again there was no pressure gauge. I filled the tyre up, but the dashboard still said I had a tyre pressure problem. Perhaps they don't bother with pressures here; just blow them up till it feels hard and leave it at that.

I asked if there was a tyre garage in Port Hardy. Yes, was the reply, it's called OK Tires. They call tyres tires here. Tired to us means worn out. My tyre wasn't worn out. It just had a small hole in it. They gave me directions. When I arrived, it was shut. It was Saturday, and they were not open at weekends. I looked round for alternative garages that were open. I found one that was prepared to repair the tyre. He directed me to an upstairs room where I sat on an easy chair while he did the job. A couple were there waiting for a mechanic to change the number plates onto a vehicle they had just purchased. They had bought a car, but greatly missed the big truck they had before, so they had returned to swap it for another truck. A pickup wouldn't work in the UK. Drive through Birmingham with it and all the stuff would be missing out of the back after the first set of lights. After an hour my car was ready and the cost of the puncture repair was $60, which was far less than a new tyre would have been. The mechanic had also washed my car and removed the cloying mud that clung to everything below the roof line, forming a layer that obscured all the paintwork. I was asked to drive the car round for a while, and bring it back to check the wheel nuts. I did this and after checking the nuts, I was happily on my way back to the Pioneer Motel.

I had a meal in the attached Japanese/Korean restaurant. Its staff were trying to interest me in Shushi. I don't know what it is about some eastern races that makes them want to eat raw protein. I believe that animal protein should always be cooked, and cooked well. There are some illnesses that can be avoided by keeping to this rule. The waitress said she could offer me what she called "White man's Sushi", which was cooked. I said, no, let's stick to something I can rely on. The thing with cooking is that it destroys germs and viruses. It also destroys the toxins that germs produce, which in the case of salmonella and botulism is often fatal without cooking. I'm not saying that Sushi is risky; it's just that if you cook protein well, it's safer than if you chew it raw. Cooking doesn't remove the radioactive and plastic waste from the fish, but at least it kills the bugs. Anyway, I chose braised beef and vegetables with rice. I don't mind substituting rice for potatoes, though it's not something I'd do myself. I like potatoes. They aren't native to Britain and various people are famed for introducing them. There are three people credited with bring the potato to Britain. They are all of the same era. There is Sir Thomas Harriot, Sir Francis Drake, and Sir Walter Raleigh. These guys were not knighted for their potato launch, and of course, the controversy as to who actually introduced them, will always be argued. Harriot was a famous scientist with an interest in astronomy. Drake was good at sorting the Spanish out, which was important as they wouldn't leave us alone. He also sailed round the globe, which hadn't been done very often then. Raleigh was also involved with defeating the Spanish Armada. Anyway, potatoes have been the staple carbohydrate in Britain since that time, and I see no need to change to rice, but I like it as a pudding. They do make puddings out of potatoes, but I've never tried it. Anyway, I had a nice bottle of Sake with my meal, and that is a good healthy drink in moderation, brewed from rice.

They have a lot of these worrying things here

Coal Harbour

13th August 2023   25031 – 25418

Port Hardy to Campbell River

21.785l = $42.89 at 25362 at Campbell River

I left the Pioneer Motel at 6am, and travelled south on the Island Highway until I found a quiet drive off the main road. Here I worshipped and thought upon the one who gave His life, a ransom for many. I thought also on life and opportunity and many good things I was able to enjoy and for which, I'm grateful.

I continued to the Highway 30 turning on the right, prior to Port McNeill. This was described on a board at the turning as a beautiful scenic drive. I followed it. The scenery once enjoyed from this road is no longer visible apart from occasional glimpses because mass forestation has lined the road on both sides for most of the way. There were two rest areas marked by signs as "Viewpoint", but all you see there is pine trees of great height. The forestry is marked out with notices of when the trees were planted. Many areas were close to one hundred years old, but most seemed to be from the 1940s onwards.

I heard that wildfires were still out of control on the mainland. The two days of nearly continuous rain in Prince Rupert had been fairly local, and dry conditions prevailed in much of Canada, and the fires were spreading alarmingly. People faced with ruin were understandably upset, and defying orders to leave their property. Not only had 25 million acres of forest burned out; there was now a human crisis. People were asking for answers. Prevention had not yet been considered apparently. Breaks in the forest to confine fires to areas were not thought to be an option. Instead, people were thinking of a national fire service that could respond with large numbers of personnel to defeat fires at an early stage. Involvement of local people instead of expelling them from the area was being suggested. They would have better knowledge of the area, and know the access points and tracks.

I arrived at Port Alice, and enjoyed the views across the fjord. The map shows the road continuing round the fjord in a loop, and though this may be the case, you aren't allowed down it. There are "no entry" signs, and you have to return the way you came. The road to Port Alice is paved all the way, but on a cautionary note, there are lots of dips in the surface, and some nasty ridges, severe enough to damage your car and lose control if you are travelling at speed. It's as well to potter along this road, and be ready to take avoiding action when the surface demands it.

I returned to the main Island Highway, and turned right to continue to my motel, the River Lodge Motel, whose address was 1760, Island Highway, Campbell River. I had entered this address into TomTom, and was interested in its idea that it was 35 miles short of Campbell River. I found out why. In the middle of the countryside with no buildings in sight, TomTom announced, "you have arrived at your destination. Your destination is on your left". It was not. There was not even a layby; only a thick forest. TomTom was really useful, and I would not manage very well without it, but frequently, it deviates from reality by a large margin in Canada. My phone is also good, but it uses Google Maps which requires an internet connection, and in a lot of places there isn't one, and if there is, it will use data unless you are in a WiFi zone. I think there is a way you can download chunks of map and navigate offline, but I haven't investigated that option.

I carried on to Campbell River, and looked round for my motel, which I found on the main road into town. My room was being cleaned, so I went for lunch, and when I returned two hours later, they were still cleaning it, and trying to freshen the air with two plug-in devices that squirted chemicals into the room at regular intervals. I don't know what sort of soap dodger had used the room before me, but clearly the level of detritus in there had taken a lot of effort to remove. I had tried the "Rip Tide" restaurant for lunch, which had been recommended by my motel. It looked nice, but pretty well all the menu options were things I wouldn't eat, or had names I couldn't understand. I tried another recommended place called "The Ginger Beef House", but there was a crudely handwritten note on the door saying that they were shut until 17th August. I managed to eat in "The Beijing House Restaurant" in the end. I chose an ordinary meal from a long list of things that I didn't understand. The waitress went round asking what everyone wanted. "Can I get you a drink?". "Would you like some water?" It was relentless. Every response to her frequent questions was "Arsum", which I assume translates as "awesome". I'm not sure why confirmation that some water was in order, is awesome, but that was the view held in here.

After lunch, I returned to my motel room and unplugged the squirty devices and went out into the garden to enjoy the river and eventually the sunset. The salmon were leaping in the river, and were being chased and eaten by a pair of seals. It's a harsh world. Most life out there is a meal for something higher up the food chain, and I guess it's something to be thankful for that we don't suffer that end very often, except being bitten by midges and gnats sometimes, and then there's always the taxman. I thought upon the plight of the salmon. They cross the ocean and then have to die at the hands of seals, sea lions, eagles, netting, and angling. Small wonder that they are in decline. The sunset was spectacular, and if red sky at night is a good omen, it would be another sunny day tomorrow.

I retired to my room, which had all my needs. My one complaint is that it was very dark. Lighting in Canadian motels is normally poor, but what made this really dim was the dark wooden walls. Hardly any have centre light fittings. They have a couple of bedside lamps and possibly a wall light. I had grown used to having no kettle, and my drinks were water, cans of beer, and an occasional coffee in a restaurant.

Sara Lake

D Lake

Port Alice

Across the sea towards Vancouver and Rocky Mountains

14th August 2023   25418 – 25992

Campbell River to Tofino and return

24.68l = $49.37 at 25835 at Port Albernie

Today was rather spoiled by roadworks. I decided on advice to visit the west of Vancouver Island. I had tried the northwest at Cape Scott, but been beaten by a very rough track. My next move west would be road 4, connecting the Island Highway 70 miles south of Campbell River to the Pacific coast.

What I did not know is that road 4 is subject to massive roadworks. Travelling from east to west in the morning, an illuminated board stated that the road would be closed from 11:30am to 1:30pm. I thought that would be satisfactory as I would be at the coast during the shut period. How wrong I was! Returning the other way, the board announced that the road would be shut from 9am to 5pm.

The outward journey was long. The road was windy with only rare opportunities to overtake. There were a few entitled people who were holding the road to ransom at very low speed. This is most unCanadian behaviour, and maybe they were some visitors. The Canadian way is to get on with it. Only the British drive like twigs in a brook, utterly oblivious to their surroundings. The frustration this caused brought on a number of utterly mad overtaking procedures, resulting on two occasions, in oncoming traffic having to swerve onto the verges to avoid a head-on collision. While such madness is not excusable, neither is the sheer inconsideration of driving a large camper van and a 4x4 towing a trailer packed with canoes close behind each other at a snail's pace. If you are one of those people who likes to make a journey last as long as possible, and you happen to be reading this, please pull over when you have a queue behind you, and let it pass. We don't mind if you've accidentally taken a double dose of mogadon, or largactil, and can't cope with your bewilderment, but those of us who have things to do would very much appreciate it if you would let us past. I followed the queue all the way for one hundred miles, arriving in an agitated state, unable to comprehend the awful behaviour of those concerned. There are many times when I want to saunter and enjoy the scenery, but I don't accumulate a queue behind me. Number one, it isn't safe to have drivers with mounting frustration close enough behind you to read the newspaper on your parcel shelf. Number two, it's grossly inconsiderate. I let them past and then everyone is happy.

When I arrived at Ucluelet, I was able to park the car for free in an undercover parking lot. This is good thinking for a place that has a lot of hot sunshine. I walked on the Wild Pacific trail round the headland for about one mile. Notices proclaimed laughably that the trail was frequented by wolves and bears, and a notice even claimed that there was a bear seen in the car park. You'd like to take these warnings seriously, but you just can't, and some were openly deriding the notices. While I'd like to say "Hi" to bears on my strolls, I didn't get that chance, and neither will you, unless you are incredibly fortunate. I think if you come across a black bear, it will be unintentional on the part of you and the bear, and all the bear will want to do is make away. Provided you don't hinder it or irritate it in some way, or try to pick one of her cubs up, you will not get clobbered. She won't waste her energy on something that doesn't represent a threat, and doesn't constitute a meal. It is believed that a black bear attacking a person will only occur one in a million close encounters. They are shy and timid.

At the end of the peninsula, an unattractive lighthouse warns shipping of the rocks. It was a bit misty and the fog horn was blowing the whole time I was there. Normally, lighthouses are of iconic shape, tall and handsome. This squat red and white structure was built in 1915, but seemingly not empathetic with normal lighthouse design. Perhaps the designers here were not good with heights or climbing a spiral staircase. Anyway, there it was, a shed with a light beam. The sea views were spectacular, and I enjoyed the walk very much.

I drove to the other end of the peninsula to a place called Tofino. This is the commercialised end, where there is literally nowhere to park. It was crammed with tourists, and any blank spaces were signed up as tow away zones. This place did not seem welcoming at all. I don't like being disparaging about a place, but really believe that in the tourist season, you are better off giving this place a miss, and you will save yourself the bother of trying to work your way through it. The place used to be nice once upon a time. Now, it's bedlam. On the return to highway 4, you drive past Long Beach. My uncle lives in Long Beach on South Island, New Zealand. It is a 3km long beach of lovely sand with hardly a soul on it, and plenty of space to park for free. The Long Beach near Tofino is not at all deserted, but the long stretch of sand is coated with thousands of people enjoying the seaside. It was very nice sand and sea, but too busy for the solitary soul.

I was looking for somewhere to have a meal, but couldn't find anything near the resort, so I made my way to the large town called Port Alberni on my return journey. I was able to order a local beer with the name of Tickety Boo, and a cod dinner with potatoes and vegetables, all for the price of $45 (about £26.50). It was a nice wholesome meal, and in view of the delays I unwittingly faced, it was a good thing.

Driving east from there, I came to the end of the queue at 4pm. At quarter past 5, the roadmen let the west going traffic through first. The queue knew they were in for a long wait. Children were playing in the road. One chap sat on his deck chair. Some young adults were playing with a rugby ball. I struck up conversations with some. They were all friendly and resigned to the situation which they said would probably be the case for the next four years. Their judgment was based on a piece of road that looked new to the west of this site. They said that had taken four years, and this piece was similar. Cyril Northcote Parkinson was not Canadian, but his view of largescale works is relevant here. Work always expands to fill the time available for its completion, was his view. I waited one and three quarters of an hour before the east going traffic queue would have a chance to roll through the scheme. Then I had a two-hour drive back to my accommodation in Campbell

River. The thing is that roadworks is big business in Canada, providing thousands of people with good jobs. In a way, it's a good thing because Canadian roads aren't allowed to decline to the potholed tracks that the UK is riddled with. In other ways, the schemes are an awful nuisance, resulting in huge amounts of lost time. They don't seem to care. In the UK, each scheme you drive through ends with a board issuing an apology for the inconvenience. They probably couldn't care less either but at least they have the decency to utter an apology, and you don't get that in Canada. Usually in the UK, each roadworks has a board with the start and finishing date on. In Canada, you don't normally get the declared end of job. It just takes as long as it takes. Schemes in the UK are normally actioned at night, so that a degree of function is possible during the normal working day. In Canada, they all go home before tea and don't come back until the following morning. Is there any possibility that night working could be done in Canada? In the UK, the men like it that way because they receive unsocial hours payments. Perhaps night work could be done to reduce the menace of Canadian road improvement schemes.

I got back to the River Lodge at 7:30pm, tired after the long day. You will see from the photos that the weather was glorious. It started off at 13C, but warmed up quickly to 33C in the day. Snow on the mountains was a reminder of their height and the much colder conditions up there.

Ucluelet lighthouse

Pacific Ocean at Ucluelet

On the Wild Pacific Trail

Kennedy Lake

Roadworks – Canada style

15th August 2023   25992 – 26272

Campbell River to Cobble Hill

19.980l = $38.94 at 26226 at Ladysmith

I left Campbell River at 6am. The glorious sunrise was already over and everything was warming up quickly. I travelled south for a few miles on the main Island Highway, and then turned left on the more scenic Ocean Route. The drive was very busy. I had hoped for quiet roads and peace with an early start. Not in Canada.

I looked for a roadside café where I could get breakfast. I saw a place that looked promising at Courtenay, but on entry, there were lots of animated conversations taking place in the servery area, and I was unable to get seated or served, and I was getting looks from various people that made me wonder what was wrong. I was washed, shaved and presentable upon inspection. Staff were doing their chores, and appeared disinterested, so I returned to my car and carried on. At nearby Royston I found exactly what I was looking for; a small popular place where I could park outside, and be served with a friendly smile inside. It's called Royston Coffee House. I had a large coffee and a scrambled egg roll. The owners are really nice and the service is excellent. Thus fortified, I continued exploring the Ocean Drive route.

Shortly after Royston, I came across a mother deer with her two fawns at the side of the road. They were almost tame, allowing a few lovely photos. Across the road was the sea and in the far distance, the mainland mountains. I imagined all the whales out there, well publicised, but less frequently observed. They say whales are often seen here and this is the best time of year. I don't know how much spare time you have, but you'd need a lot of it to see them. Anyway, the view was very pretty and this coast is well worth a visit.

Moving south, I drove through many villages and towns on the Ocean Drive. It was quite built up all the way, apart from a few short stretches of countryside and forest. I visited three BC ferry terminals. One was a small concern that provided a service to Denman Island. I walked along a wooded trail from the ferry, parallel to the shore, ending with a nice view to the island. The next ferry I viewed was the Departure Bay ferry which I would be travelling on in a couple of days. It seemed to have access, and I hoped for trouble-free travel for my early morning departure. The third ferry I viewed was the Duke Drive ferry that goes from south Nanaimo directly to Vancouver city, whose high-rise skyline could be clearly seen from the terminal.

From here I made my way on back roads to Cobble Hill where my good friends Don and Kim live, who I have met several times during voluntary work in Cambodia. It was a great thrill to meet them in their home country, Canada. I arrived at 4pm and we had a jolly good catch-up. Then we repaired to Cowichan Bay for a restaurant meal, which was lovely. The pub had an outside balcony where we sat overlooking the small harbour. Don and Kim had kindly offered accommodation for two nights, and had dedicated tomorrow to show me round the area.

Black tailed deer Royston

Cowichan harbour

16th August 2023   26272 – 26272

Cobble Hill, Chemainus, and Victoria

I breakfasted with Don and Kim in their lovely home, in its super setting with views over the countryside to the mountains.

Don drove me to Cowichan Lake. On the way we saw a black tailed deer suckling her fawn. The lake and outflowing river were very scenic. We watched a strange craft making its way across the lake to the shore where we stood. It was like a floating caravan, which is exactly what it was. It was homemade, and sat on a twin hulled keel. The owner happily explained all the features to us. He was well kitted out for a happy time on the lake. He also had a vehicle with adapted trailer to move it to another area if the need arose.

We moved on to Chemainus where we viewed a large number of murals throughout the town on the outside walls of buildings. All were wonderful paintings, but wouldn't have been my choice for the living room. The subject of many of them was the hard work and conditions that made this area profitable. Of course, we as workers realise that profit and riches come to the owners. Those who do the grafting are paid as little as possible, and that wasn't much in the early days. Even today, the disparity between worker and owner is vast, but the fact is that without the labour force those at the top would not be able to achieve anything. You only ever hear about the top one. For example, Thomas Telford built canals, roads and lots of national infrastructure in the UK. In fact, he didn't do any of it. He was the man at the top, designing and communicating with the government. Every shovel, pick, and barrow were operated by men earning next to nothing, and working in unimaginable hardship and danger, without any mechanical aids. What do we know of these men? The answer is nothing. We know that they generally died young and in poverty. Thomas Telford in contrast had nice circumstances and is remembered as a national figure of importance. He is remembered with statues and even a large town is named after him. I'm not sure he would have been particularly proud of the town, its housing estates and thousands of traffic islands. He would have probably been more interested in its former prominence in the coal, limestone and iron industry.

Anyway, Chemainus depicts the logging industry for which the area is famous. A little museum exhibits many photographic plates from the late 1800s up to more recent times, again mainly of logging and saw mill work. Some revealed the social side of the community, but life must have been very hard in those days.

We lunched in a restaurant on vegetarian paninis and soup before returning to Cobble Hill to pick up Kim, and drive on to the island capital, Victoria for the afternoon. As cities go, Victoria is lovely. It isn't too big and overgrown for itself, and the older infrastructure has been sympathetically preserved. Canadian documented history, like the USA, is fairly short compared with the UK. However, the predominant UK history that those in the north American continent are so interested in, is largely a testimony to how bestial people are. Most of it is a history of war and violence. It really isn't anything to be proud of. The only buildings preserved are castles, which people built to protect themselves from violence, trebuchets, bows and arrows. From their turrets were poured such loveliness as boiling oil and molten lead upon the assailants. Our history doesn't make nice reading. The sadder fact is that the world doesn't learn from history. It just uses its ability to make more fearsome ways of dishing out death, and using them to take over other nations, or defend against such aspirations. Why folk can't contrive to live in peace and mutual support, is difficult to comprehend, but perhaps if they hadn't scythed through each other's countries, the global population would have been even larger and unsustainable than it is today.

I visited a number of notable buildings in Victoria. One was Murchie's Tea Shop, displaying and offering teas and coffees from all over the world, and smelling wonderful. The beautiful Munro's bookshop had a stunning exterior and interior. It had just the sort of ambience that made you want to sit down and study. The parliament building was admitting visitors, and we decided to enter. A man outside told us that we should carry on up the steps as he was not waiting in the queue. We followed his advice, but as we entered the door, we were swiftly ejected by a security guard as only a few were admitted at a time. No more could be admitted until a number had been discharged from the back door. Once our slot became available, we went through security similar to the airport. We were divested of most things, but were allowed to wear sufficient to protect our modesty, and our belongings were all X-rayed. We were scanned too. Once inside we were allowed to photograph and wander round the beautiful building. Of particular interest was the chamber which is similar, but smaller than the House of Commons. They don't feel the need for over 600 MP's here, nor of a second house with over 700 in it. The legislature was not sitting, so we were able to have a good look. Also, the central area with its beautiful domed roof was amazing. Many stained-glass windows were wonderful and extolled the character and noble values that are far distant from many of the political decisions and politicians that we are familiar with today. Outside was a statue of a young-looking Queen Victoria. The monarchy is being considered a lot in Canada. Many spoke to me, asking what I thought on the subject from the UK perspective. Many older people had huge respect for Queen Elizabeth, but what the bank notes of the future will look like is up for discussion.

Outside the parliament, we enjoyed an ice-cream in the hot sunshine and watched the sea planes coming and going, and a lot of small ships. We then drove past the main Vancouver dock where the cruise ship, Queen Elizabeth was berthed. From there we continued through an outer suburb where the rich of Vancouver live and each house is considered to be worth millions of dollars. While folk have those sums in their banks, and wish to live there, those property prices will continue to soar.

Then we moved on to Buchart Gardens. These huge and beautiful gardens were built in a disused quarry in 1904. They have had time to mature and even the trees have grown to their adult size. It is a truly wonderful place, whose central arena is like the Dingle Garden in Shrewsbury, but on a massive scale, and is surrounded by many other themed garden areas. At one end of the garden is a magnificent waterfall, whose patterns are like a floral dance, and which is lit up at night. The individual garden areas merge together delightfully. Areas include a Japanese garden where ferns and water play an important part. There is an Italian garden laid out with attractive but formal beds and statues. A Mediterranean garden even had banana plants, but you have to be realistic about the prospect of fruiting when you are this far north. There were beautiful fountains in this area. There was a dahlia garden with blooms of a huge size and of excellent quality. The only area that was not quite so good was the rose garden. Very large, with examples from all over the world, the plants looked a bit sad with yellowing leaves. The roses just didn't express the same feeling of vibrance and happiness that were thrilling throughout the rest of the gardens. A woodland area had sequoias and Douglas firs of huge size. The largest specimen was planted in 1937 and was of terrific height and girth. These trees are in their prime at 86 years old, and can live for a couple of thousand years if idiots with chainsaws are kept well away. Many specimens have survived in California where these venerable giants are preserved. We finally walked to the main fountain again to view it lit up. It was spectacular.

We drove back to Cobble Hill, full of the beauty that we had enjoyed together. I holiday alone and enjoy my experiences, but what a joy it is to do these things in company, sharing viewpoints and commenting on things together. We are social animals, and even though one is alone, most of us crave the companionship that an evening like this one brings out.

Chemainus mural

Victoria parliament building

With Don and Kim at Victoria harbour

Buchart gardens

17th August 2023   26272 – 26481

Cobble Hill to Whistler

I left Don and Kim at 04:30 and drove to the BC Ferry terminal at Departure Bay. The short journey of 47 miles was not without incident. Although I had allowed plenty of time, two sets of roadworks caused delays, even though no work was taking place. Road workers tend to pack up and go home for the night. Unfortunately, some signs were confusing. My TomTom is sunk when the road is shut. You perform the detour asked for by the workers and TomTom thinks you have made a mistake, and starts asking you to do a U-turn. Another of its knavish tricks is to ask you to continue up the side turn you have taken, and then bring you back by a circuitous route to the starting point of your detour. As I neared Nanaimo, a sign directed me to turn right for the Departure Bay Ferry. I did so, accepting the sign, despite thinking it was too early for the turning. The sign was incorrect. I realised the error quite quickly and turned back to the right route.

I arrived at 05:30 to a state of chaos. Very few staff members were on duty, and the queue was backed up onto the main highway. A man seemingly about to have a seizure of some kind was agitatedly darting about giving conflicting instructions to the drivers. He said only one ticket booth was open as staff expected had not turned up. Progress was incredibly slow and there was a lot of impatience and crossness being ventilated. As I got near the ticket booths, a second one opened and things started to improve. I got through and parked in Lane 4 and watched the dawn. I boarded the boat at 06:15, and it was soon underway for the two-hour trip to Horseshoe Bay, which lies on the mainland north of Vancouver.

The queues for breakfast on the ferry grew rapidly, and I decided to give this a miss. I wanted to enjoy the views and scan the sea for possible orca sightings, and spending an hour in a breakfast queue is something I can do throughout life, if I really try to find a place with a huge clientele. The opportunity to enjoy a lovely morning on the sea was too good to miss. The views to the mainland mountains were spectacular. To the right lay Vancouver with lots of high-rise blocks, speaking eloquently of stuffing, claustrophobia, discontent, and crammed living accommodation. We see these cityscapes across the world, and it is evidence of over-population. I met a wealthy man who disagreed with my view on this. He said it was obvious that when things got crowded at street level, you go upwards. When you look at the Manhattan skyline, he believed that such things spoke of the prowess of design, and the fact that a lot of space in the sky remained usable as living areas. I found out that he lives in a very large area of parkland with its own deer and scenic beauty. He is one of those who preached an idyll that we should accept, but he didn't have to or even want to. This is the thing that places many politicians in an unsuitable position for their role. They are so far beyond the lot of the commoner, that they cannot grasp the reality of normal life, and cannot empathise with it, or alleviate problems with sensible decisions. One's view of others tends to be moulded by one's own situation. An extreme example is that we will happily wipe out whole colonies of bacteria with a Detol spray, but if we were to be a bug, we would detest the advancing bottle, and the one holding it. The feeling is similar to that we have when someone in charge exacts yet higher taxes that squash our style, but the one in charge can easily pay out of their pocket money. We aren't meant to live like caged animals, in zoos and farms, so why is it acceptable to coop our people up in this manner in high rise blocks with no garden.

The boat docked at Horseshoe Bay, and I was soon on my way to Whistler, where I had booked a night's accommodation in the Aava Hotel. There were many pretty views on the way, but the road developers seemed to have gone the extra mile to prevent you stopping to take photos. Many of the laybys were on the left-hand carriageway with barriers or signs to prevent you from legally crossing the road to gain access. I tried turning right a few times and crossing the carriageway on bridges, but parking was almost impossible. I had limited access to capture the scenery. This is where a drone would be useful. You sit in your tree lined or house lined layby, and send up one of the ever more popular drones to gain the view you wanted from the sky, up above the world so high, like a drone in the sky. They are becoming popular enough now for the authorities to ban them in many places. As yet, they still offer a solution for views they deny by road rules and structures built or planted in the way, provided you don't launch them near an airport or other installation specifically banning them.

I reached my accommodation in Whistler and checked in. By this time, it was hot and sunny. There is a parking lot underground belonging to the hotel, and I paid another $22.50 to use it. The authorities have sown up the parking situation in Whistler. It teems with tourists in Summer and skiers in Winter, and they capitalise on the situation. Anywhere that looks like an opportunity to park for free, has a tow away notice fixed somewhere. You pay your money and take your choice. I just left the car underground where it stayed cool for a couple of days.

I looked for a place to have lunch, and selected Stonesedge restaurant. I saw no stones or rock face there, so we just accept the incongruous name of the place. I had a salad with a small salmon steak perched on its summit, and a drink, the cost being $45. I asked for the best vantage point to see the black bears which I had been told roamed the streets. I was advised to go to the golf course, which is where the bears hang out, they said. I looked for signs to the golf course, but saw none. I asked for directions, but found that golf is the thing everyone does in Whistler apart from skiing, and there are three golf courses round the town. I made for the one offering the most remoteness. I found that the only way in was through a staffed entrance. They weren't up for sight-seers, and said there were no bears there. They said I should go to the gondolier, and on the way up the mountain, I would see the bears wandering underneath. I'd heard this one before. The only fact connecting bear sightings with the gondolier is the price of being winched to the summit and back, which is about $80. I walked round the golf course on a trail, and this was a lovely walk. Though signs warning of bears everywhere, the truth is that the whole Whistler area has 60 bears, 15,000 humans, and three million tourists per year. These statistics give you the relative chance of seeing bears, locals, and people from across the globe. Whistler is not named after the human ability to form their mouth opening into a small round hole through which air is blown. There is a little animal called a hoary marmot that lives here that makes a whistling sound, and that's how the town got its name.

I continued on the trail until I reached a body of water called the "Lost Lake". It was not at all lost, and is clearly marked on the map. In what sense it is lost, is unknown to me. The lake is tranquil and lovely. No doubt, bears, moose, elk and caribou hang out here, but I didn't see them. Neither did I see the archaeopteryx, unicorn, or dodo, but never mind, it was a lovely walk, frequented by scores of people who were swimming, boating, biking, or walking. I did see some wildlife that was new to me, and which I identified as a Steller's Jay. It shares the unfortunate behaviour of other jays we are familiar with in the UK. This behaviour is the ripping out of small birds' nests and eating the young. The Steller's jay was not as brightly coloured as ours, but was a beautiful blue and grey.

Returning to my hotel, I booked a bear safari trip in a Landrover for two hours in the morning. I tried to book the 6am trip, but could not because they needed another two people to fill the vehicle. They only go if the vehicle can be filled. There is space for seven in the Landrover in three rows. For the $185 + 15% tip, you get picked up from your hotel, and my trip was at 9am, with hotel Aava pick up at 08:50.

Leaving Vancouver Island

Browning Lake

Mount Tantalus

18th August 2023   26481 – 26741

Whistler to Clinton

17.703l = $35.39 at 26515 at Pemberton

I prepared for the bear safari, packing my bag, and checking out of the hotel, apart from gaining permission to leave my car underground until the afternoon. Then I sat in the hotel foyer and waited for the Landrover. It came for me just after 08:50, and then went on to the next hotel to pick up a couple, booked in the name of Nicola. The driver asked the lady waiting outside if she was Nicola. She replied, yes. She and her partner got in and off we went to the third hotel where another Nicola was waiting. The first Nicola already on board was the wrong Nicola. She was booked onto a bear safari, but with a different company. There's a lot on this game. We drove quickly back to the previous hotel to drop Nicola and her partner off, and picked up the right couple from that location. Then we returned to the third hotel to pick up the family from there.

At last, we were on our way. Our first leg of the trip was a mountain track on Whistler where we travelled a few miles through berry bushes loved by bears. We turned off on side shoots down minor tracks, and even with eight pairs of eyes, we saw none. Then we travelled to a more distant trail that went up to Callaghan Lake, the stated objective being to gain more height as the cooler air would possible be more amenable to the bear's psyche. It was all to no avail as far as bear sightings were concerned. We did see some beautiful scenery, and we all received a good massage from being bumped along tracks for a couple of hours. Our driver regaled us with increasingly unlikely tales of his bear sightings which more than matched any fisherman's tales for likelihood. We all listened in good humoured politeness. Those in the back used an interval to start singing, "if you go down to the woods today, you're sure of a big surprise".

People will always postulate why a bear safari or a fishing trip has been unsuccessful. They will tell you it was too hot or too cold, too wet or too dry. The simple fact is that there was a "y" in the day, even though there wasn't an "r in the month". There will always be bear stories, and they are nearly all macabre or filled with huge peril. The fact is that many true black bear stories backed up with videos, give testimony to the affable and curious nature of these animals towards humans, rather than their aggression. I'm not telling you what to do, but I will tell you what I'd do if I happened to get close to one. I'd keep calm and still, and take lots of photos, and wait until it walked away. I wouldn't squirt it in the face with bear spray for two reasons. First, I refuse to carry the stuff, and secondly, it's nasty stuff to squirt about. There are a lot of photos and videos available for you to do your own research, and you will find that as far as black bears are concerned, the grave threats are mainly of human origin. These beautiful animals should be respected, and loved for their intelligence and good looks. Black bear attacks are extremely rare, and normally occur if you have a dog with you. I can tell you the story of how the Wrekin and the Ercall in Shropshire were formed. It involves a huge giant and an old cobbler. At this point, you've probably switched off, so I won't bother you with the rest of it. Bear stories told by guides who are trying to make up for no sightings, are about 98% poppycock.

There are similar stories for the other large animals of Canada. The collective noun for moose is still moose, in the same vein as the plural for sheep. I was told by a lady that her son was out on his bike when a large moose came out from the side of the carriageway and raced down the road at the side of the boy. They kept looking at each other. It ended when the boy got worried and stopped, letting the moose win the race.

Anyway, we did see a beautiful waterfall called Alexander Falls. Also, we viewed a spectacular mountain top named "The Tusk" from the prominent vertical rock on its summit. The trip soon came to an end, and we returned to Whistler, and each itinerant was returned to their hotel. I picked up my car from the parking lot at Aava, and drove north towards Clinton. The route was declared by a couple to be a dodgy steep road with hairpin bends. Compared with mountain passes in the UK, France and Switzerland, this was really tame. Its maximum gradient was 10%, and at all times there were two lanes, and it was passable by trucks of all sizes. I send a welcome to Canadians to visit the Wrynose Pass in the Lake District, England, with its 33% gradient. Obviously, you'd have difficulty in a Yukon or Dodge, or RAM, because you'd have no idea where to point it because you wouldn't see the road over the bonnet. All you'd see is the sky on the way uphill.

We digress. I reached the summit of the mountain pass and continued to Clinton. I had difficulty finding the Caribou Lodge that I had booked for the night. I had fed the address into TomTom, which had decided that this lodge was in Cache Creek, and told me I had reached my destination when I got there. As there was no Caribou Lodge where it told me, I asked for directions, and nobody knew where it was. I headed to Clinton, 36km away, and asked again when I arrived. My TomTom is great at finding towns in Canada, but rubbish at finding addresses. It really does have its moments, but it is an invaluable tool. I checked in and had a meal in the restaurant within the lodge. I asked for fish and chips which was the special of the day. I asked if there were any greens with it. I was informed that the answer was no since it was a special. I explained the five-a-day thing that we have in the UK. She hadn't heard of that. As a favour, she brought out a bowl of salad to go with the fried meal.

On the walls of the restaurant, I counted 20 large animal heads, some of them were moose. I don't understand men. They like to fight and kill. When there is a war, they often volunteer to go and shoot the other side. When there is no battle going on, they choose to shoot other creatures instead of people. This is one of the reasons why herds of caribou no longer roam the countryside. They are more solitary these days.

I settled into my accommodation. I had Room 109, on the ground floor of a two-story block. I was at the end of the block, which was pleasing as I could hear noise from above, but only on one of the sides. Next door was quiet, but it was as if the missing herds of caribou were blundering around upstairs. The din was hideous. At 10:30pm, water started dripping fast through the light fitting on the bathroom ceiling. I didn't fancy confronting the life upstairs as it sounded to be caused by primitive and dangerous types. I walked round to reception, but found it deserted, locked, and in darkness. The water deepened during the night, and it was a paddle to get across the bathroom to use the toilet.

Alexander Falls

Bear searching

Callaghan Lake

Callaghan Lake

19th August 2023   26741 – 27143

Clinton to Blue River

18.493l = $33.45 at 26845 at 100 mile House

I packed up at Clinton and left the pervading wetness of my room at 6am. I wrote the owners a brief note to let them know where the water was coming from, and deposited my key in the key return box. I pressed on northwards to 100 Mile House where I filled with petrol and bought a sandwich from the Coop for breakfast.

Then I returned briefly south until I reached Highway 24, where I turned left and travelled alongside a number of lakes, stopping to take photos at some of them. Of particular interest was Green Lake, which was not green, but was shrouded in early morning mist. It was cold at this high altitude, and a heavy frost lay on the ground, and my car temperature gauge registered zero.

I visited the chasm at a place appropriately called Chasm. It is a huge canyon, supposedly ripped out at the end of the ice age. The glaciers and polar ice, are all that remain of the ice age, and some of them are retreating. Many would like the ice age to return, and fondly think that if we stopped burning fuel, this would start to happen. I'm not sure of the validity of the arguments. What I do know is that they have caught on, and have formed a lovely platform for governments to base green taxation on. I also believe that if it started to get significantly colder, people wouldn't like it.

Highway 24 offers a lot of lake and swamp scenery, which is quite pretty, and also the type of terrain loved by moose. I saw none, but a cute little chipmunk sat on a rock enjoying a nut, and gave me a photo opportunity. These little guys are hard to photograph because they dart about so much, but this one appeared unbothered by my presence, and had a favourite nut in its front paws. Another lovely spot is Bridge Lake Resort with a great store where you can enjoy a well-priced mug of coffee, and have a nice chat with the staff, who are knowledgeable and friendly. It's a quiet spot, far from the madding crowd, and the peace was delightful.

At the end of Highway 24 at Little Fort, I turned left up Highway 5. I turned left again to visit Spahats Falls, which were spectacular. The torrent rushes through a very narrow gorge before plunging down to the river below. The impression is that the water shoots straight out of the rock face. The falls are well worth a visit.

I continued north up Highway 5 to Blue River where I had lunch at the bear safari that I had visited a few weeks earlier. I chose beef stew, which could either come in a bowl, or a hollowed-out bread roll. I chose a bowl, but it still came in a hollowed-out bread roll. Salad is also provided. When I last came, the material was presented in a bowl. Either they've broken them, or settled on the economy of the bread roll bowl versus the much larger porcelain bowl. Never mind; it was fine.

I decided to stay at Blue River for two nights, as my accommodation was lovely, and the hosts were great. This seemed a nice opportunity to enjoy a relatively smoke free atmosphere before travelling back towards Vancouver. My room was an individual log cabin which was self-contained, and very peaceful. The hosts had nicely decorated it and tapestries hung from the walls. Although this décor wasn't my style, it indicated a level of care that has been absent from the more common utility accommodation that I was used to.

I walked and drove all round the village, hoping to see bears that were said to frequent the village. One local told me to visit the refuse dump at dusk, when he said I would see several. This turned out to be the black bear equivalent of a red herring. There were none. The views of the mountains and Blue River are lovely, and there are quiet grit roads to explore to get off the beaten track and not be bothered by the rushing traffic.

The noisiest feature of Blue River, is passing trains. The train itself is quiet enough, but Blue River has six crossings which have no barriers; only flashing lights. The train drivers vent their horns copiously at the approach to each crossing, and the 143dB blast avoids any possibility that you might be unaware of a train coming.

Chasm at Chasm

Early morning mist at Green Lake

Bridge Lake Store and Café

Spahats Fall *Blue River lodge*

Blue River lodge

20th August 2023   27143 – 27482

Blue River to Mount Robson and return

24.323l = $43.76 at 27304 at Valemount

I left my Blue River cabin at 7am and drove north towards Valemount, until I came to a small grit road on the left. This was a logging track, unlikely to be used on Sunday. Here I pulled in and worshipped, remembering Jesus in the way He appointed. Seldom will people give their life for others, but we remember Jesus who God sent, that whoever believes in Him will not perish. Here is hope of the most wonderful kind. It was blissfully quiet, the only sound being the gurgling of the river below me.

I continued down the grit road until it came down to the river, and gave pleasing views in either direction. It seemed an ideal spot for moose, but they'd all been eaten. I returned to the main road and drove onwards to Valemount. I passed several moose warning signs on the route, confirming that this was ideal territory for them, but as you cannot have your moose and eat it, there were none to see. Moose stories abound in this area. I've told you the one about the moose racing with a boy on his bike. Here's another, related with such seriousness that it made me laugh. They don't like it when you don't believe the stories, especially when others are present. Here it is. There was a herd of moose in the road. Really! A driver was impatient and sounded his horn. One moose was angered by this display of frustration. He walked round to the side of the car, fixed his antler under the sill of the car, and flipped it over. The story was amusing, but far-fetched. I don't know what the car was. It could have been an Isetta, I suppose, that would make it more believable than a Yukon Denali.

In Valemount, I stopped for an egg muffin and a mug of coffee, and filled my car with petrol. Then I continued northwards to the junction with the Yellowhead Highway. Here I turned right towards Mount Robson.

At Mount Terry Fox, I stopped to view the mountain recently named in his honour. He was a remarkable young man who sadly died from cancer at the age of 23. He initially had an operation to remove his right leg, following which he determined to run across Canada to raise money for cancer research. He never finished the run because the cancer spread rapidly to his lungs, but he raised a huge sum of money, and is remembered with much affection. At Mount Terry Fox, I met a Mr Austin, who had climbed the mountain yesterday with Terry's brother, and many others who were continuing the fund-raising efforts. It is amazing how some respond positively to their illness, and become an inspiration to others.

I continued to Mount Robson, and walked from the carpark up to Kinney Lake. It is a 5km walk each way, but the views to Mount Robson, and of the lake, are wonderful. The day was very calm, and provided beautiful reflections of the mountains in the lake. It was a hot day, but at the higher level by the lake, it was cooler and refreshing.

I returned to Blue River Cabins after my walk, and had an evening meal at Sandman Inn, which is the surviving restaurant at Blue River after others have closed their doors in the downturn during the Covid lockdown. I had a salmon steak which was very nice. The lockdown was very successful at stopping business in the UK. People here quite liked the idea of not going to work, and tried to continue with it long after it was no longer necessary. The thing was only possible because the government paid everyone to stay home. Of course, this soon racked up an enormous debt, which those who benefitted from were not required to pay back. The bill has to be paid at some point by increased taxation, and those who did not benefit because they were working in essential services, or who were not working for some other reason, also will have to help pay back the debt. The stay-at-home initiative was so popular that it started the "work from home" concept, and this really caught on. NHS management and many others who were not needed at their workplace, decided to stay home. This brought them the benefit of not having to travel and also, they received payment towards their household bills. A portion of their council tax and energy costs were met. You can imagine how much work got done by these managers. It was a well-known fact that they used the unscrutinised time as an opportunity to go shopping or to spend time with friends and family. Many times, they were seen out enjoying themselves. As long as a train of emails emanated from their computers, this was sufficient evidence that a sterling work commitment was being achieved by these frequently unnecessary roles. Anyway, in Canada, people were required by law to remain close to home, and the restriction prevented tourism, and this resulted in the closure of many businesses. Government edicts related to covid, had far reaching and unforeseen consequences that exceeded the viral illness in many ways. Covid in most cases followed a mild course and full recovery was achieved in a couple of weeks. Some had much longer periods of illness, and the "long covid" syndrome was coined to name those so afflicted. It was found to be predominantly an illness of those with good sick pay schemes. The self-employed did not seem to suffer as much. Many people suffered the huge life changing loss of businesses and loss of loved ones who had succumbed to the illness. The mental effects were massive. Unpleasant circumstances will always be turned to advantage by some. Hence the saying, it's an ill wind that blows nobody any good. Those who provided masks and other personal protective equipment made fortunes. So did big pharma companies who provided vaccines and other antiviral medication. Two companies were making $1000 per second out of their products. Human nature being what it is also extended these financial benefits to those who invested in these things. What more opportunity to invest did those in authority have than to steer contracts towards companies they had an interest in? All this was going on in the UK while those at an ordinary level had, and still do have a tough time of it.

Mount Sir Allan MacNab

North Thompson River at Cedar Creek

Mount Terry Fox

Mount Robson

Kinney Lake

21ˢᵗ August 2023   27482 – 28097

Blue River to Banff

24.515l = $38.22 at 27794 at Jasper

I left my cabin at Blue River at 4am. This sounds really early, but I had a long drive and wanted to have another look for wildlife in the Jasper area, and wanted to arrive there early while the wildlife was still roaming about. Reasonably priced motels are not a feature of Jasper, so if you are wanting to budget, you have to sleep further away. Banff accommodation too, is ridiculously priced, but I managed to book a room in the YWCA this time. There is no reason for these excessive prices. I refuse to fuel what I see as racketeering. You would find that if everyone boycotted these establishments, it would stop the nuisance almost overnight. As long as people pay the exorbitant fees, the motels and hotels will charge them. The facilities at these expensive places are no better than at cheaper places further away. The water and electricity are the same. Soap and toilet paper are the same. Paying $400 or more for a bed for the night is not the best use of one's cash. So it was, that I was committed to a long drive on occasion. The thing with pricing policy is that some owners will charge what they think people will pay. This is a wrong strategy. You should cost your establishment carefully. This will include consumables and staffing. Then you need to make a profit, but it's the size of that profit that distances a wise and decent owner from a greedy one.

I particularly wanted to see a moose in the wild and my opportunities were fading fast. I decided to revisit Lake Malign and walk to Moose Lake before people had arrived in large number. As all these creatures tend to be shy and shun human company, early visits are essential. At Moose Lake, people speak of "the" moose. Adult specimens are around 800kg, and are too big to miss. You might miss a mouse in the long grass, but something nearing a ton, you can't. They speak of the moose as if it is the only one. Anyway, I arrived at Moose Lake in time to see him. A small group of people were watching him from the opposite side of the lake, and they were whispering quietly to each other. They had no need to whisper. The moose had already spotted them and was walking away. He wasn't being particularly quiet, and was sloshing his way through the shallows to get further away from the humans who had turned up and disturbed his feeding time. Whispering was unnecessary. Moose was on his way. Normal talking would have been fine. I was overjoyed at the opportunity to see him, though at a distance, and I took a few photos.

I completed the moose loop walk back to my car. It was a cool start to the day, and the pervading smokiness prevented the sun from heating the place up. It did not achieve more than 21C all day despite there being no clouds. This confirms the truth of what they say about it being colder after a volcanic eruption, or other sky pollution. People talk about a nuclear winter that they believe would result from the pollution of a nuclear blast, preventing the sun from getting through. A major volcanic eruption temporarily cooled the earth by 1.7C in the 1800s. For me, the disappointing thing today was the diminished scenic views. Everything was smoky. Due to the rather late and feeble attempts at putting the wildfires out, the situation seemed unlikely to improve any time soon. The attempts at present are concentrated on trying to save properties. The fires are still raging today, and said to be out of control. Aerial dowsing is not successful because the smoke is so dense that the helicopters cannot see the fires. So far, 26 million acres of forest have burned out, which is an area greater than the size of Holland. The largest single fire that is now spreading into the USA, is 170 square miles in size. The amount of soot and CO_2 put into the atmosphere exceeds all the vehicular pollution, and makes a mockery of the zero carbon initiatives that get talked about in august assemblies by folk in expensive suits.

I stopped at a wayside café for some beef stew and a coffee, that were served extremely slowly. It does not sound a time-consuming job to ladle some material from a vat, and to pour a coffee from a machine, but here, they make a science of it. I eventually arrived at Banff at 4pm. I found my room in the YWCA to be fine, but basic. The large room had a nice comfortable bed and a wash basin. The floors were like mezzanine, and gave the impression that you were in a Victorian hospital. There was a communal bathroom down the corridor. At $260 for the night, it was substantially cheaper than the other hotels and motels. Is it worth doubling this price for a room with a private en-suite? Only you can decide. I did, and that's why I was in this regency accommodation with its clinical atmosphere. It was just fine for me. I was actually in the room for about 10 hours, of which, 6 hours were spent in the bed. This works out at just under 50 cents a minute for occupying this space.

After settling in I walked to town for an evening meal. I tried a few places, but they looked rather full and noisy. I found a restaurant that was in an upstairs room, that seemed to be quieter. It was The Elk restaurant. The room had a balcony overlooking Mount Roundle. Here I had fish, chips, and salad. The fish was coated with batter, a sort of case hardening that is used to give the fish a more substantial look, and makes a nutritious dish into a highly fattening one. I usually crack the batter off and leave it on the plate. I only eat the fish, which on this occasion, was of a decent size and thickness, and I really enjoyed it. Often batter is used to make a minute piece of fish that has been thinly cut by surgical means, visible to the naked eye, but in my restaurant, the fish was lovely. The entertainment while I was eating it was provided by a flock of sparrows, who were eating the hanging basket flowers on the balcony. It was interesting to note that they seemed to prefer the yellow blooms.

I walked back to the YWCA slowly, taking in the Banff evening atmosphere. There were thousands of tourists there, intent on a party type evening. However, there were lots of older couples who seemed to be trying to recreate the time of their youth when arm in arm they strolled down the street talking of times gone by, and sharing elegance and regency charm. The nearest you could get to this in the UK would be a Victorian spa town like Bath or Cheltenham. It was quite pretty with every establishment vying with each other for the best show of flowers.

Sunrise

Moose

Sparrows enjoying the yellow blooms

Mount Roundle

22nd August 2023   28097 – 28501

Banff to Creston

21.340l = $38.18 at 28240 at Radium Hot Springs

I woke up at 6am to a soaking wet morning, and it continued to rain all day. I hoped that this would help to dampen the wildfires, but I heard later that the rain did not venture as far as western BC. One blessing is that the rain had laid the soot and smoke that pervaded all the sky yesterday. The visibility was only poor today due to the rain and mist. The pollution had largely gone, and it was easier to breathe, and the back of my throat was no longer irritated by the smoke.

I set out at 7am, firstly for Johnston Canyon, northeast of Banff. On arrival, it almost stopped raining, and I set out on my 7km walk to the falls and back. However, at my furthest point from the car, it started to rain heavily, and I was well soaked by the time I reached the car again. The falls were spectacular with the glacial melt added to by the rainfall. I visited the lower falls first before continuing to the upper falls.

I was glad that my outward walk was early in the morning as it appeared that a large percentage of the population had decided to visit these falls, and were arriving as I finished photographing the views. My return walk was difficult on account of the number of people coming the other way. It was like swimming against the tide. The walk was not without humour. Those in charge of the place had decided to nail lots of notices to the trees to stop people from wandering off the trail. Then in case people decided to ignore the notices, they had erected a very strong metal fence the full length of the walk. Further than all this, they had set up remote monitoring to enable detection of anyone breaching the fence. You'd expect this sort of sophistication surrounding Buckingham Palace, but not a waterfall in rural Canada. It seems this was all in the name of helping to preserve a declining black swift colony. That's fine, but how much disturbance to the swifts was caused by the erection of all this fencing, notices, and remote-control equipment? Swifts tend to nest high and not be particularly worried about human presence. Hence, members of the swift family nest on people's homes, even above doorways. I find that most wildlife just wants leaving alone. Manicuring and controlling the habitat they have chosen is probably unwise.

When nearly back at the carpark, which was now full of a huge number of vehicles, there is a restaurant. I thought a coffee and sandwich would be nice, but the sandwich packs available in shops and filling stations for $5.69, were $10.48, so I gave them a miss. It isn't that you can't afford two rounds of bread cut diagonally to make two sandwiches, and packed with some sort of filling for 11 dollars. It's the principle of encouraging prices like this by falling for them. You won't suffer by waiting a few minutes until you get to the next filling station, and getting your sandwich there, so that's what I did.

I soon reached Radium Hot Springs, where as usual in Canada, you can't get at the water where it bubbles up through the ground. This would be really interesting, as it is in Iceland, and some places in New Zealand. In Canada, they've controlled it all. They've erected buildings over it and ducted the water into swimming pools where you sit and enjoy the warm water in a manicured commercial setting. You can't help wondering if your entrance fee goes to paying the electricity bill for a boiler. I did check the water coming away from the site and it was really cold. Am I to believe that the hot water coming out of the ground is enough to keep a pool supplied with hot water? I don't know, but I'd like nature to be displayed as it is. Once you turn it into the complex that they have done, you have all sorts of control measures to keep the pools free of verruca, and fungus. Anyway, I'd like to see hot water coming out of the ground rather than visiting a resort where nature is hidden under a building complex. Well, tough, this is the way it is!

I continued into the village and into a café for a pot of coffee and a snack with a price tag of $35. I chose to come to Canada, of my own freewill, so I cannot complain that prices are rather high. However, I cannot help making comparisons with home in the UK where I have a decent breakfast and coffee for £6. Here it's nice, but I've just paid £21 for the same thing. I filled up with petrol here.

Most of the roads today were declared by roadside signs to be wildlife corridors. We can all agree with this provided we define what is meant by wildlife. I think they mean moose, bears, and that sort of thing. They were not in evidence. However, the term wild means untamed, aggressive, unrefined, and even savage. When I saw the standard of driving today, I could not help agree that these roads are wildlife corridors. The heavens had opened and driving was hazardous with lots of surface water. I slowed to 90kph, which was as fast as I felt it was safe to travel. The rest of the traffic was bent on roaring by at their usual speed. A large truck thundered past, closely followed by an unmarked police car, that suddenly lit up in blue, yellow and red flashes. The truck driver's reign of glory had come to its end for that day.

A little further on, emergency crews were still playing hoses on a huge caravan that had been towed by one of those enormous pickups. The whole combination had been burned out, and only a skeleton structure was left.

At Fort Steele, I spotted smoke in the distance, and wrongly thought that I was approaching another wildfire. It was a steam engine. I drove past and parked at Fort Steele station to photograph the train coming in. Despite the rain, it was a lovely spectacle. Steam engines evoke all sorts of memories, and they are living things, hissing, smoking and having lots of visible moving parts. The only thing they can't do is reproduce. In every other respect they are alive. They eat coal, get hot inside, and move. This locomotive was number 1077, one of Canada's oldest at 100 years. It was originally used in the logging industry, but is now operated purely for tourism.

I continued through the very large town of Cranbrook, and on to Creston, eventually arriving at my motel, the Creston Valley Motel at 4:30pm. I checked in and then walked to a nearby pub for my evening meal. There was no obvious door into the pub, and the one I spotted round the back led into a Cannabis shop. The sweet smell was strong when I opened the door and walked in. This is all legal here. I explained that I was looking for a meal in the pub. The chap said, it is next door, but it's fine in here. I didn't think so, and left. Once in the pub, it was as if everyone had already been next door. I couldn't get served, so I left there as well and walked back to my motel. Here I picked the car up and drove to a nearby restaurant called the "Real Food Café". It was novel and nice to find a place where real food was considered important in contrast to fast food. I ordered fish, rice, and vegetables, and even went for some homemade cheesecake. The bill was on the high side, but with my holiday drawing to a close, I felt that a little treat was in order, and the food had been lovely.

Johnston Canyon

Upper falls

Fort Steele railway

23rd August 2023   28501 – 28957

Creston to Grand Forks

17.155l = $30.00 at 28639 at Nelson

I left Creston Valley Motel at 7:30am, and headed west on the Crowsnest Highway. The sky was dark and lowering, and soon the rain started. Much of it was very heavy with a little hail and the occasional thunderclap.

The first leg of my journey today was to Salmo. There were lots of ravens at the roadside, hoping for insect kills no doubt. Soon the road started to climb, and at the first summit was an area known as Kootenay's Fairy Forest. I walked in and found the trees adorned with hundreds of artefacts and memories of loved ones. It seemed to be an iconic place where people would come and fix stories of love, tragedy, and even pictures of those who have passed away. I came away with a feeling of melancholy, but people feel some solace here, spending time in memory. A homeless lady, wrapped in foil blankets completed the picture of the troubled living amongst the memories of those departed. The forest is a lovely calming place with a warm atmosphere. For the present, those of us alive, have further opportunity to do our best, and happily enjoy the wonders we are surrounded by.

Soon after, I reached Kootenay summit which is 5820 ft above sea level, and on the summit is Bridal Lake. Why it is so called is a mystery, but it was lovely, and you could sort of imagine a happy couple posing by the water before descending the mountain to start the more mundane aspects of married life; doing the dishes, or whatever!

I continued to Salmo, where years ago gold prospecting drew many people in hope of making their fortunes by discovering nuggets of huge value. Logging became a large industry with lots of props needed to support the underground workings. It's a bit of a nuisance if the tunnel falls in, and the wooden props were a great benefit. The railway was built to provide transport into the area. Gold has always been a valued commodity. It has little use as an engineering material as it is too soft. Its huge value is down to its enduring nature. We can dig up gold objects that have been buried for millennia, and once the clay is washed off, they are as good as new. Most other metals corrode away when exposed to the elements. People have always hankered after gold. Personally, I've always had more mundane things I need. You can't do anything with gold, apart from look at it, and that's never seemed an attractive thing to do. A box of gold sovereigns would just be a worry. Travelling to beautiful scenery on the other hand, is not a stealable asset. The experience is in your mind rather than being in a tin under the bed.

Next, I reached Apex summit at 3143 ft. Though these summits are high roads, you don't notice the climbs because the gradient is gentle and the roads are wide and easily reached by the largest trucks. Years ago, this was not the case, and poor tracks were the only way in. The railway became very important, and still is as far as freight is concerned.

Then I arrived at Nelson and crossed the huge Kootenay River by the bridge and headed up towards Balfour, and historic town that was probably named after Arthur Balfour who was the British prime minister in the early 1900s, and responsible for the Balfour Declaration, to allow the Jews to return to their ancient homeland after nearly 2000 years scattering worldwide.

Approaching the town, there was a long delay due to resurfacing work. I stopped to photograph Kootenay Lake and the Blaylock Mansion on the opposite side of the road. This mansion is a fine period property that was owned by the renowned Selwyn Blaylock, who was an inventor, involved in the smelting industry. He was also involved in the Allied war effort. He did extremely well for himself through hard work and application of his intelligence. He had this mansion built to his own specification. It's certainly a fine property.

I continued to Kaslo, and then turned left on the mountain road towards Retallack. This mountain pass was one of the most peaceful roads I've driven on in Canada with only occasional traffic. It was a joy to drive for once. On top of the pass, I noticed a strange low structure of maybe 100m. I stopped and found that it was an open tube constructed to channel migrating western toads, a species in decline here. Are they doing the right thing here marshalling toads into tunnels? If I was a toad, I'd want leaving alone thanks. Anyway, it was interesting seeing the toads making their way along the channel constructed for them. The migration is an annual event.

Next, I drove over Poulson summit at 5036ft, on top of which was a weather station. It's interesting how the weather has become the subject of much scientific research, and yet, is unpredictable. Forecasts are often completely wrong even in the short term. Long term forecasts are notoriously pointless. Anyway, stations at many strategic places gather data, allowing comprehensive graphs to be maintained, to see emerging patterns. The only predictable pattern is that summer and winter, day and night, cold and heat, never cease. Within that pattern, conditions vary hugely, dependent on many factors. The best predictors are the outdoorsmen who have been in a locality all their lives, and know what each sign means. Apart from that, I look out in the morning, notice what is going on, and adjust my activities accordingly. Most of the weather forecasters go in the same vein, telling you what they are noticing when they look out of their windows, and what their weather stations are picking up. A small bit at the end tells you what they think will happen on the following day.

I finally arrived at Grand Forks, where I had booked a night's accommodation at Johnny's Motel. This was built in the 1950s. I checked in, and then repaired to The Station Pub for an evening meal. News of the wildfires was on everyone's lips. Stories abounded of properties burning, and of people being ordered to leave rather than fight the fires to save their homes. The thing that remained uncertain was how I was going to get from here back to Vancouver for my flight home. Some roads were closed, and had guards to ensure that people didn't venture down them. Other roads were not guarded, but had closed status, only permitting residents to drive out. The news was that the fires were spreading southwards into the USA, and the northward spread was stalled. For the moment, my route west on Highway 3 was open.

The authorities, supported by the media are increasingly angry because people subject to evacuation orders, were not leaving their homes, but were staying to defend them from the fires. Conditions were generally warm and dry, and fires had spread at lightning speed. One feature of all sorts of different problems is that "experts" are very common. Their views are sought and published, and the public are expected to heed their advice. Too often the "experts" turn out to be opiniated, but lacking in knowledge and wisdom. Firefighters have been thin on the ground and woefully inadequate in comparison to the magnitude of the task. It is therefore very understandable that people would stay put and try to protect their property and their livestock, rather than leave everything to the fire's consumption. Heroic stories of people being successful in preserving things from the fire gave encouragement to others to do the same.

I guess you will soon hear the epithet, "we are learning from these events". How often have we heard this sentiment from politicians trying to claw back some credibility from disasters that were eminently avoidable had the right steps been taken. Often the right steps are pointed out by those on the ground, but are ignored by the authorities who later try to get it accepted that the events that overtook them were new and not experienced before, and now they would never happen again. As far as the fires are concerned, I venture the opinion that much more needs to be done to prevent fires. It's all very well crowing about the equipment and expertise we have to deal with a problem, but if we can stop it happening in the first place, so much the better. In that vein, we know that logging is a huge industry. How about logging in corridors that split the forest into sections? How about removing all the dead trees that are dry kindling ready to spread a fire quickly? How about aerial and satellite scanning of the forests to allow immediate intervention when a fire starts? How about a large reserve firefighting force, that can be called up immediately should the need arise. How about including local people in the reserve force as their knowledge of off-road routes for access would be very valuable?

I settled into Johnny's Motel, and had interesting conversations with my next-door neighbours who were regular visitors, and had seen the changes over the years. One of the changes was the huge increase in traffic. Another was the flood risk. I was here at the end of a warm dry summer. There are wet periods when the river overflows. For now, it was nice to sit on a chair outside the back of the motel and enjoy the river. One of the great passions of Canadians and Americans is for British history. The most recorded history you get on the American continent is back to the 1800s. Before then, things are not documented. In contrast Britain has documented history for a very long time. Most of that history is so gruesome that you feel revulsion at it. Our history is filled with brutality, barbarism, and is as far from civilisation as light is from darkness. Nearly 3500 years ago, Moses received the ten commandments which are the guiding principles for life from God. Jesus, 2000 years ago, made the point that everything hangs on the first two commandments which are that we love God and love the neighbour. Those critical of the message asked who the neighbour was. The reply came that the help for a wounded and robbed man came from a complete stranger, and the critic was asked to go and do likewise. History is a record of how much we love the neighbour. And very often, that's not much. History is a record of how much we want what our neighbour's got, and if we think we are powerful enough, we'll take it by force. Anyway, the amusing thing about the desire for British history at Johnny's Motel is that as you drive in, there is an old red phone box in the drive. I looked at it and did a double take. I'm only up on telephone boxes because I wanted one, and I know the various design changes down the years. If you want one in the UK, you can adopt one for a community project where it stands for £1, but if you want to make a feature in your garden out of it, you have to pay several thousand pounds. The one at Johnny's, was not quite right, so I went to the reception desk and asked about it. This one was made in China! You'd never have known if they'd paid more attention to detail. The right dimensions and features are readily available, and it's as easy to make it right as wrong.

Bridal Lake

Mirror Lake

Slocan Lake

24th August 2023   28957 – 29236

Grand Forks to Princeton

17.785l = $33.06 at 28959 at Grand Forks

I left Johnny's Motel, Grand Forks at 7:30am, and with only 150 miles to my next stop, I was able to take it easy today. I had booked the Ace Motel in Princeton for tonight. I was to travel very close to one of the largest wildfires today, and there were mixed reports on road closures. The town with a question mark over an evacuation order was Keremeos, which apart from being in Canada, you'd think was Greek from its name. The whole area is known as the Okanagan, and the authorities are asking people to stay away. I had to pass through it on my route to Vancouver, and a very large detour would have been necessary to avoid it. My worry was that road blocks may be set up. In fact, I found the whole area relatively smoke free compared with some that I have passed through. I found it fairly quiet too, perhaps because many were avoiding the area. The sky was a beautiful blue, and settled weather was forecast for the next few days.

    I came to Osoyoos over the mountain pass, and from the east, I had a wonderful view over the city from my high vantage point. Here, a sign declared that Osoyoos has Canada's Warmest Welcome. I didn't stay there long enough to prove this statement. I parked by the sign to view the city and surrounding area, and then snaked down the mountain pass and across the Osoyoos Lake Narrows on the bridge, and drove through the city.

    After Osoyoos, there were lots of vineyards and orchards for cider apples. There were lots of other fruits like strawberries, plums, pears, and many others growing and being sold in wayside sheds, from this fertile area. I stopped at one cider house to buy a glass of cider, but was told that they were not allowed to sell it by the glass. I could buy bottles. I thought that was strange, but hey, that's what you find in a different country. In the UK, they'd pour cider into any container you brought, and charge you for the volume. It isn't difficult to buy or drink the stuff, which actually is made for that very purpose. It isn't made to look at. Anyway, they gave me some samples. That was legal. It was jolly good. Then they gave me directions to a place down the road where I could buy a glass of the material, but when I got there, a crudely written sign on the door stated, "out of all cider". I survived on the samples.

    Outside, there was an abundance of fruit and vegetables, and no doubt, it was all quality stuff. There is just a little snag. You get the same thing in the UK when you go to a farm shop. You get the idea that when you go straight to the grower, you cut out the middle man, the shop, or the supermarket, and therefore, the price should be cheaper. Think again. If you are on a budget, buy your food from the Coop, or whichever supermarket is the cheapest. It was a very warm sunny day, and I decided to invest in an ice cream. The prices weren't displayed, and that's usually am indication that the price is going to be high. They know that once you've taken the ice cream out of the freezer and presented it at the till, you are more or less committed to buying it. Mine was a small kit-kat, and it was $5.25. I sat outside the market and slowly savoured every microgram of that ice cream. There was no cash back on the wrapper, so I put it in their bin. At least part of the $5.25 would go towards recycling the wrapper!

This area was unlike most of Canada. Rather than dense forest, this was an area of wide-open valleys, used extensively for fruit and vegetable growing. The mountains here were only thinly covered with trees. Wildfires cannot take hold here as the large gaps have far greater resistance to fire spread than dense trees.

When I reached Hedley, I found a lovely museum of local history, and enjoyed two mugs of fine coffee and a homemade apple pie. The museum had no visitors as everyone had been asked to stay away from the area due to wildfires. Locals viewed the restrictions as an over-reaction, and said that the risks to this area had been exaggerated. Anyway, I chatted long on a wide range of subjects with these lovely people. These delightful occasions are the opportunities needed to find out what goes on behind the scenes. You find out how people feel about their environment, and what their joys and worries are. At present the nearby wildfires are the main topic of conversation. There is the heroism of those who have stayed put and saved their properties and livestock from encroaching fire. It is widely held that instead of booting these people out, it would be far better to use their skill and local knowledge. After all, these people have managed their own wildfires for generations, and know better how to deal with local situations than the "experts".

Regarding reports, I tend to make my own mind up on things based on what I see. Therefore, I incline to the view that fire in this particular area has been exaggerated. This area is not thick forest, and fire spread would be difficult. Any fire would be easily accessed and extinguished here. The huge fire which is a fact, and terrible, is the other side of the mountains from Keremeos.

At Carson, I did drive to the USA border, and spoke to the guards to discuss a possible future trip to the USA. They were very helpful, and provided all the paperwork I needed. While I was there chatting, I was horrified to see a large Winnebago crash into the barrier. Granted, it was a huge vehicle, but if folk want to try and pilot a holiday home of that size, they need to practice on a disused airfield somewhere, rather than inconvenience everyone on the public highway with their lack of talent. People with no spatial awareness try to drive cars, and the result is nerve wracking for many of us. But when they get behind the wheel of a Winnebago, they pretend that it's the same as their car. It just isn't, that's all.

After Hedley, I took the "Old Hedley Road", which for 20 miles parallels the new Highway 3, but on the north side of the Similkameen River. This road was beautifully quiet, and I was able to drive slowly and take in the views without being in anybody's way. I could hear all the frenzied roaring of Cummins diesels across the river, but I was alone and content. I saw an osprey in a tree top by the river. Ospreys are more common here than in the UK, but it was lovely to see and photograph this bird. I had heard of other nests in different parts of Canada, but this was my first sighting. Sighting is always better than hearsay. The white breast was unmistakeable. Nearby, a coyote was quartering a field, no doubt looking for lunch.

Most of the properties here are made from timber, locally sourced. Around 30,000 houses are made from timber each year in Canada, I'm told. This doesn't sound a great number, but you build houses to meet your need. In the UK, some leaders want hundreds of thousands of houses built each year. This need is only because around half a million immigrants settle here each year, and they all need houses. This huge population increase in a country which is well up the global table in terms of population density, I leave you to judge. In contrast, Canada is 41 times bigger, but has half of our population. That is sustainable. Canada can support its population in terms of food and fuel, and can easily be self-sufficient. The UK imports over half of its food and fuel. While this works in peacetime, it doesn't in time of war or other situations that slow global transport. Our supermarket shelves would empty in days. That is the stark reality that eludes the politicians, who are so far removed from reality as to lack the ability to comprehend it. Anyway, timber homes are very common in Canada. They are nice, and can be warm, but the downside is that they catch fire more easily than brick properties. The future of timber houses in Canada hangs in the balance as officials are saying that new properties must be fire resistant, and wood isn't. You can paint it with fire resistant coatings, but it still burns when you get it hot enough. Brick doesn't burn. Bricks are made in a kiln at 1000°C, and can laugh at burning trees. However, other parts of buildings are flammable, such as roof timbers, windows and doors.

At the end of the Old Hedley Road, I was almost in Princeton. I turned right into the town, and it was only a few yards to the Ace Motel where I had booked a room for the night. This was a nice motel in nearly every way, but the reception staff recommended that I didn't drink the tap water. I thought that this was a bit strange, as Canada has good quality tap water. I checked and found that Princeton water is unfit for human consumption, unless you boil it. A new water supply is being provided for Princeton, but at present, it is not to be drunk. All I had in my suite was one of those ridiculous coffee machines that doesn't boil water. It gets hot after about half an hour, but it doesn't boil. I made a cup of tea with water about 70C, and hoped for the best. The coffee machine is almost invariably what you get in a motel in Canada, despite it being far inferior to a kettle. I know that instant coffee is not the coffee aficionado's dream, but for a brew that is ready in two minutes, a kettle and a sachet of Nescafé beats these silly coffee machines hands down. It's a bit like sliced bread which was invented in 1928, nearly 100 years ago. Some people still don't buy sliced bread, and some people still live in caves. But come on, give us a kettle that will boil the water, especially in Princeton where that's what you are meant to do.

I had my evening meal in "The Copper Pit". Unusually for Canada, the meal was lovely. I had potatoes, vegetables, and a salmon steak. It was a real meal, good and wholesome. I walked to and from my motel and was thrilled to see a black tailed deer up close. These lovely animals come into town in the evening, and they seem unafraid of people. I was able to approach quite closely and get a few nice photos.

Wilgress Lake

Osoyoos

Apple growing, Keremeos

Hedley Museum

Osprey

Black tailed deer

25th August 2023   29236 – 29410

Princeton to Hope

I left Ace Motel, Princeton at 7:30am, and tried to find a place open for breakfast. This quest was unsuccessful, so I went into the "Save on Foods" supermarket and invested in a pack of egg sandwiches and a bag of grapes. There is something to be said for the life of a tramp, as promoted by Robert Louis Stevenson – "Bed in the bush with stars to see, Bread I dip in the river". However, as cheap and cheerful as the vagabond may be, creature comforts are programmed into us as nice, or even, necessary.

I continued on Highway 3 until I reached Sunday Summit at 4206ft. There was nobody about, so I had the huge parking lot to myself. For reasons best known to the highway's agency, a sign asked you not to stay there longer than 15 minutes. I stayed there for 20 minutes to see what would happen. Nothing occurred and nobody came. I asked myself why it was called Sunday Summit. I couldn't figure it out so we have to let it be. Here's an interesting fact though. A Canadian will try to figure something out, whereas we will work it out. On a similar note, a Canadian will go to check out a viewpoint, whereas we will go and have a look. We would expect the police to check something out if it appeared suspicious, but if you stop at a viewpoint, you aren't checking it out; you are enjoying the scenery. If an Australian turned up, he'd ask you how you were going. Your answer would be, I'm not going anywhere yet, but I'm doing fine; how are you? The way different countries express themselves is interesting.

Anyway, I continued downhill until I reached Mule Deer Campground. I saw no deer, but a new find was a Cedar Waxwing, a delightful little bird feeding on berries in a saskatoon bush. At this site was a short trail to what was said to be a beaver lake. Not only were the beavers absent, it looked as if there had been no beavers there for a long time. The view across the lake was nice and it was very peaceful. Some mallards were enjoying the morning sunshine. Chipmunks were darting about.

I moved on to my next point of interest, which was a mountain pass, which had a lookout over the USA border, to the mountains beyond. A topograph showed the names of all the mountains, and this was a very nice touch. Unfortunately, the view was somewhat spoiled by smoke in the atmosphere. Although the shapes of the mountains were clear enough, there was a blue haze over everything. Of great interest were a few chipmunks and a Clark's Nutcracker, all of whom were hoping for food. I was saddened when a carload of humans who had originated in the far east turned up. Their two young children got out and immediately picked up stones and aimed them at the chipmunks. I was appalled that the parents did not stop this outrageous behaviour, and I had to intervene to do so. If we don't teach our children to love and respect nature, what sort of people are we turning into? Cruelty is horrible to see. This behaviour sharply contrasted with the next car that turned up. Two little girls got out who were thrilled to see the chipmunks. Their dad gave them a couple of peanuts each, and with patience, the chipmunks took them from their hands.

I continued uphill on a grit road to the top of the mountain. I assume that the vehicular access was provided to reach a large communications mast at the top. There was a car park and a trail extending in two directions. I explored them both. Again, I saw birds that I hadn't encountered before. First, there was a grouse of a larger kind than in the UK. Next, I spotted warblers feeding in the vegetation on the ground. A bit of research identified them as Adubon's Warblers, a regular visitor to western Canada. It was a pleasure to see these brightly coloured birds.

I returned to Highway 3, and my next stop was Sumallo Grove where I walked through some very large cedars. These majestic trees have obviously been here for a long time. They are well known, and I had been advised not to miss seeing them. Trees of this height and size overawe us by their presence. In comparison to the centuries they live, we are very finite. Some trees are the nearest thing we can grasp to explain eternal life. As the Bible puts our hope – "as the days of a tree shall be the days of My people". Some trees can live for thousands of years.

My final stop was at Hope Landslide where a massive slide of rock and debris destroyed a few kilometres of the main highway, and four people lost their lives. The jumbled rocks remain to this day. The slip is thought to have been triggered by a small earthquake. We are all subject to the powers of nature, and can never be fully prepared for the catastrophe they can bring. The mountains here are very steep sided, and daily send rocks crashing onto the roads. Roads passing next to steep rock faces are normally signed as no parking zones. When you drive through, you will probably be ok, but if you park your car there for a few days, the chances are it will be a different model to the one you left. The larger rockfalls tend to be in the spring. During winter, water in cracks in the rock freezes and expands. When the thaw comes, the rock is let go from its face and crashes down to the valley below.

I entered Hope and checked into my accommodation for the night, which was the Best Continental Motel. This was next door to the Rolly's Restaurant where I had an excellent evening meal.

I took a stroll round the town, and was interested to see a large mural on the end wall of a building. It had been painted by Ken Skoda, depicting his view of the vitality of eternal life. It is described by the prophet Isaiah in chapter 40 v 31, as the eagles mounting up on their wings, and as being capable of running and not being weary or faint. It is a lovely piece of art, carried out in acrylic. It is a picture not only of vitality, but harmony.

Having an interest in railways, I tried to find Hope Station. I looked on the rail website and the train times and ticket prices were given. I could have bought a ticket to Vancouver. The website gave me the opportunity to purchase it, but I'd never have caught the train because the station was disbanded years ago. Governments like to be thought of as bringing progress. I'm sorry, but depriving communities of public transport should never be thought of as progress. The fact is that as people have grown more affluent, they now have private transport. Their dad gave up the horse for a car. Now they have several different cars to choose from. They stopped using the train long ago, so the government or rail operator, closed stations down. Once stations close down, they get converted to other uses, and eventually the whole line gets closed down. Once that infrastructure is lost, it is almost impossible to open it up again. While there's plenty of gas, and money, people aren't going on the train, but when the gas runs out, people will be sorry that the train is no longer there. I guess in Canada, they can easily reinstate a station in Hope, because they have left the line in place. In the UK where the whole line has gone to the scrap metal merchant, and someone has built housing estates where it used to be, they will have to buy a horse and cart. Our government decided that an answer was to build a brand-new high-speed railway from London to Birmingham, and continue it northwards to Manchester and Leeds. There are just a few problems with this flawed thinking. One thing is that we don't all live in London and Birmingham. Even if we did live in those places, we might not want to transit between them. I only ever met one person whose aspiration was to live in Birmingham, and he had a mind problem. All that HS2 was ever going to do, is get you from London to Birmingham a few minutes quicker than it would take on the existing lines. The massive cost of the project, and the devastation it has caused is so ridiculous that there can only be vested interests that have kept it going. When it was obvious that most people viewed it as a white elephant, they decided to invoke an independent review. The only thing is it wasn't independent at all because its chair was a previous chairman of the project and of a major engineering company. You couldn't make it up, could you? By the way, a white elephant is a polite description of something large, expensive, and not useful. It derives from the time when they would give these rare and expensive animals to monarchs in Siam. Those rulers could flounce about on the things, but they never did anybody else any good. The point with national projects in the UK is that the chequebook is left blank. The project managers know this, and each project ends up several times more costly than the planned price, and you and I pay for it while the investors and project managers treat themselves very well.

Chipmunk investigates my shoe

Mountains in the USA

Sumallo Grove

Mural - Hope

26th August 2023   29410 – 29772

Hope area

22.575l = $43.55 at 29412 at Hope

I left Best Continental Motel, Hope at 8am, and looked for a café for breakfast. I was unable to find one, so I filled up with petrol and bought a sandwich from "Save on Foods" supermarket again. Then I continued to Merrit on Highway 5. Highway 5 turned out to be the fastest piece of road in the whole of Canada that I have driven through. Someone has decided that its speed limit for this unique length of tarmac is mostly 120kph compared with 90 or 100 kph elsewhere, with occasional stretches of 110kph. People decide these things. We have a difficult character in Wales who has made speed decisions at the opposite end of the scale, and inconvenienced a lot of people. I tried to find an old parallel road that I could wander along, but was unable for some time, so all I did was turn off at each junction, and have a look round for points of interest.

My first turn-off was at Coquihalla Summit. I noted that the height was 4081ft. A grit road went further uphill through a mass of roadworks where they were laying a high-pressure natural gas pipeline across British Columbia. Once past the roadworks, I parked at the summit and walked onwards to Falls Lake. It was a nice walk, and though signs warned of bears, I saw none. A group of lads were camping by the lake, and they said they had seen a bear at 2am. I'm not denying that, but they had a well-drained bottle of whisky with them, and I've known people's ability, achievements, and experiences to be considerably, though fictionally enhanced after consumption. I stayed at this lovely lake for some time, watching trout leaping. Though it was a hot day, it was refreshingly cool by the water. I walked half way round the lake, but was unable to get further on account of dense undergrowth.

I returned the few kilometres to my car and drove to a viewpoint overlooking Merritt. It looked to be a large town or city. I was still looking for an alternative route to Highway 5. I set my TomTom to Aspen Grove as my next destination, and the route criteria to shortest distance. This is often a recipe for off roading. TomTom conducted me up an old road that is full of ridges and potholes. At least it was very quiet. At the side of the road, I was privileged to see a marmot sunning itself. I managed to get a photo of this cute animal, about the size of a small cat. The marmot is a type of ground squirrel.

Next, I came to a memorial for Laurie Guichon, a rancher in the area who wanted to establish a grassland reserve. Well, he got his wish, and this grassland is named after him. Here, I spotted a dead tree with an osprey nesting on its top. The mother had one chick who could fly. The mother went off for food and the chick set up a loud and continuous cheeping. Then it got fed up with waiting and flew off. It didn't go far, and soon returned to the nest. The grassland reserve was lovely, and supports much wildlife that requires this habitat. It makes a nice change from mass forest.

I had some good views of Allison Lake on my way back to Hope where I was to spend my second night in the Best Continental Motel. I had my evening meal in Rolly's restaurant again.

Thus ends my mountain views and exploration of Canada, as tomorrow, I have to drive to Vancouver, and ready myself for flying home.

Falls Lake

Allison Lake

27th August 2023   29772 – 30000

Hope to Vancouver

22.964l = $44.53 at 29867 at Abbotsford

I left Best Continental Motel, Hope at 7:30am, and bought a sandwich and cake from Save on Food" supermarket. Then I travelled a few miles to a quiet gravel road where I could worship.

Then I walked to Bridal Veil Falls, which was beautiful despite low water flow. The falls are not supplied by glacial melt, and the flow is directly influenced by rainfall, which had been quite low this summer. The woodland trail to the falls was also lovely, the huge trees giving a cool atmosphere under their shadow. As is normal in Canada, a large number of signs told you what you could not do, and the penalty for disobedience. There were areas where you couldn't park your car, or it will be towed away. Don't walk beyond the sign, or we'll fine you a lot. A few people were giggling at a sign which told them that a bear was in the area, when clearly, there was not; except of course for the one on the sign.

I continued the short distance to Vancouver, but was too early to check into my accommodation. I detoured to Capilano in north Vancouver, where a suspension bridge is a notable attraction. The bridge is a long one for foot traffic across a canyon. They charge you $8 to park your car, and $68 to walk over the bridge. This had been recommended to me as a good place to visit. In addition to the bridge, and included in the price, you can traverse a skywalk, fixed between trees and a huge height. There is also a cliff walk fixed to the side of the rock face. These arrangements look William Heath Robinson in style, and appeal to the daring do. However, I'm past that stage of youth, and prefer to walk on Terra Firma. I don't mind how high the surface is as long as it's been there since the beginning. Prancing on bits of timber a few hundred foot above a river, is not my idea of joy, especially when the arrangements are fixed up on flimsy looking wires and struts. To the uninitiated, it may be fun, but when you've studied metal fatigue, strain, and stress, you tend to think what could go wrong, however improbable. Edward Murphy in 1949 penned the law, "if something can go wrong, it will go wrong". Though this was 1949, it had already been noted a number of times previously, that things tended to go wrong. So eventually that bridge, across which people swing from side to side, will go wrong, and the whole caboodle will be pitched into the abyss. Of course, proper and regular inspections and replacement of worn parts, can greatly reduce the risk, but it's still a finite risk, and one which I don't enjoy taking.

I did cross the bridge and go round the cliff walk, and report that the views were stunning. However, it looks and feels perilous. The whole venue is designed to rake in a lot of money, and it was doing very well at it. They don't advertise it as a money-making venture, but as an educational experience, where you can learn the value of nature, particularly the trees and the water.

I'll guarantee that the educational side of things didn't work today. Most people there came for a thrill, and a number were using what strength they had, to make the bridge swing uncomfortably. The message the owners were trying to convey was water conservation. As far as treated water is concerned, there is a cost in processing it. As far as natural water supplies go, the cycle was noted through King Solomon 3000 years ago. He pointed out that water coming from the sky, enters the rivers and seas, from where it is taken again. Therefore, water cannot be wasted as such. Whatever we do with water, it is part of that cycle of evapouration, cloud formation, and rain. You can drink water, wash with it, water your plants with it, but it is part of a global cycle, and the total water volume is fixed for ever. You can split it into its two component gasses, hydrogen and oxygen, but as soon as you strike a match, there is a loud bang, and you have your water back.

The education continued to lecture on lichen, which some people pronounce as liken. Whatever you decide to call it, lichen grows in roughly circular patches. They were saying that lichen depends on clean air. Well let me tell you that I don't believe them. Lichen patches grow on tomb stones in Birmingham cemeteries, and if there's anywhere that doesn't have clean air, it's there. Anyway, perhaps it grows better in clean air than dirty air. At the time of my visit, the air was probably as dirty as it ever gets, as it is full of soot, smoke, and CO_2 from forest fires. The amount of pollution is hard to comprehend with our finite minds. Millions of tons of pollution are in the atmosphere of most of Canada which is the second biggest country in the world. The idea that forest fires are natural needs to be reconsidered. However natural they may be, they are not the best thing when they get out of hand. And, when they get out of hand, they cannot easily be stopped. Have a little bonfire every now and then if you want, but a bonfire the size of Holland is taking it too far. Canada has water bombers which take scoops of 2600 gallons from lakes in less than a minute, and drop them on the fire. That's a lot of water to drop on your fire. They haven't been able to deploy these very much because the smoke has been too dense and widespread to see where the fire is from the sky. I can think of another good use for these water bombers. Imagine 2600 gallons of cold water on a street protest! It would return with another lot within 5 minutes. That would dampen the ardour of such folk. They wouldn't hang around for long.

Anyway, I enjoyed the canyon scenery and forest, and then made my way through Vancouver to my accommodation. It's called MeiXue, which sounded Chinese. I looked the words up, which apparently mean "beautiful snow". Snow is beautiful provided it's over 5000 ft up a mountain. It's lovely to look at, but not lovely to try and make your way through to achieve your everyday tasks. It's fine in childhood days when responsibility doesn't extend beyond building snowmen and throwing snowballs at each other. Once that white fluffy stuff curbs your ability to carry out daily tasks, it becomes a nuisance rather than a beauty. It's great on picture postcards, and distant views. Hopefully, that's what the owner of MeiXue had in mind.

I had a little difficulty gaining access because there is no reception, and the owner lives elsewhere. However, an email was sent to me today, giving the access code to the hall of the property, which is a large house that has been modified to self-contained suites. Fantastically, mine had an electric kettle, a simple contrivance that has been missing all across Canada. Now, I can have a mug of tea or coffee in a couple of minutes.

I drove to the harbour for an evening meal, where out of the array of fast food, fiery spice and raw fish establishments, I found a proper restaurant called Kove Kitchen. I think they meant "Cove", but they've spelt it "Kove". I had chicken breast, vegetables and potatoes, which to me is a proper meal. They'd gone to the extra trouble of marinating the chicken in something, and coating it with something else, and I could have done without that interference. Why some people can't keep meals simple is beyond me. I like meals that comprise meat or fish with vegetables and potatoes. I prefer no embellishments, coatings, marinatings, drizzlings, spicings etc. Life is made worthwhile and interesting by what you do rather than by assaulting your internals with chemicals. To me, eating isn't a science. It's a way of assimilating the essentials for life. It should be done as simply as possible. I've never understood professionals who use every available utensil in the kitchen in order to furnish a meal. Just whop everything into one vessel and boil or roast it as long as necessary, and then eat it. By the way, you convey the completed meal to your mouth with a knife and fork. This invention hasn't got to the east yet where they still use knitting needles, which they call chopsticks. Over here we chop sticks to light the fire with, not to eat with.

After my meal I strolled round the harbour and found a boat with a few vacant seats for a whale watching trip tomorrow. I booked a seat. It was a bit expensive, but guaranteed. Of course, wildlife is not guaranteed. It's safe from the company's point of view because they know full well that you are on holiday, and the free trip they offer in the event of no whale sightings, cannot be taken up. There have been two trips out today, and the itinerants have seen many humpbacks, orcas, and sea lions. I asked if they had seen any mermaids, and they said, no. I think a better way to charge for these expeditions, would be to charge for the boat trip, and charge separately for whales spotted. One whale would only count as one, even if it kept popping up and down like a yoyo, as they tend to. You can always tell which whale it is. The sea is a violent place. Anything that has lived in it for a while has chunks nipped out of it, which leave scars. Each whale, and there aren't many, has characteristic markings, and they are all named. Each different whale close enough to observe with the naked eye would count as a sighting.

Having booked my place on the trip, I returned to MeiXue for the night, where I had a comfortable bed and room, and a kettle that really made the difference.

Bridal Falls

Capilano Suspension Bridge   *Capilano Cliff Walk*

28th August 2023   30000 – 30008

Vancouver

I left MeiXue at 8am, and bought sandwiches for my breakfast, and for the whale watching trip. Then I went to the harbour to find a parking spot, since available places very quickly fill up during the tourist season. By the time I had parked in a free all-day place, it was 9am, and I had 3 hours to use before my trip.

I sat in the car and had my breakfast, and then went into "Blenz Coffee". I guess "Blenze" is a skit on "blends", but that would bear your research. It is a Canadian chain of coffee outlets. Anyway, I ordered a coffee, and then noticed a water colour artist working at one of the tables. We got talking. His name is Ted, and he showed me many examples of his work, which was fantastic. It included many portraits of visitors to the coffee shop, as well as scenery in BC, France, and Spain. I spent a very happy hour with Ted, and was amazed at his perception and quick lines to achieve a likeness within a few minutes. He really has an amazing talent.

Then it was time to walk to Seabreeze for my adventure on the ocean waves. The itinerants gathered, and we were given a safety briefing, and then we were under way. The harbour was calm, but once outside, the water was choppy, stirred up by an easterly, and the passing of many large boats, or vessels as they are often called. Why call a boat a vessel? A vessel is a container for holding fluids. The only time a boat is filled with fluid is when it hits a rock, and that's bad news. Let's stick to boat and keep things simple. You might have a vessel in the boat, and you might have water in the vessel, or rum if you expect the need. We headed for Vancouver Island, and went round a few islands on the way. We looked all round for humpbacks and sea lions etc.

The company has a fairly failsafe mechanism that normally works. If the trip comes up with nothing but salty water, there are a couple of resident orcas who have set up home in a small area for the last 20 years or so. When nothing else was doing, we made a beeline for their hangout, and they came up trumps as usual. So, we did see a couple of orcas on our whale watching trip, and it was quite a nice boat ride. The two orcas were hunting in their island archipelago including Galiano Island. A few whale watching boats were in the vicinity, all clearly in the know, and were all making their money from these two residents. The orcas were Jack and one of his siblings, whose name I can't remember. Orca is a posh word for killer whale. I guess it sounds nicer. People think of an orca as a friendly creature they can play ball with, but the reality is that while they are generally friendly towards people, they are big powerful predators. Jack and his brother are the two orcas we saw today, and are fixtures in this area throughout their lives. It was wonderful to see them at reasonably close quarters as they surfaced and dived, sometimes together. It was a lovely opportunity.

Most whales are regarded as gentle plankton swilling giants. Few of us have seen them because they try to keep away, especially from Japanese and Norwegian whale catching teams who decimate their numbers by harpooning them. These two countries appear to have little regard for the preservation of these wonderful animals.

There was a slight issue on our way back to Vancouver. One of the engines developed a strong heavy vibration that shuddered through the boat, and the driver turned the power down. It appears that some debris had been drawn into the propeller. Once this was removed by the onboard engineer, we were under way again, and were soon back to the harbour.

I had my evening meal in Kove Kitchen again, where the waiters were pleased to see me and hear my tales, and see some photos.

Then it was back to MeiXue for my final night.

Orca

29th August 2023   30018 – 30030

Homeward bound

9.53l = $19.81 at 30023 at Richmond

I left MeiXue at 08:30, and as my flight was not until 19:45, I decided to go to the harbour and spend a few hours by the sea. Having arrived, the weather decided against my idea. Conditions descended to very heavy continuous rain with thunder and lightning. It was relentless.

I had breakfast in the car and readied my paperwork and belongings for the airport. The forecast offered no improvement during the next few hours, so it seemed sensible to fill the car with petrol and drive to the airport. I filled up at a Petro Canada station. Here's another thing. Petrol in eastern Canada is $1.35 per litre, but it gets more expensive as you travel west, and in Vancouver it's $2.10 per litre. There seems no good reason for this disparity, but we have to accept the way it is. It's still a lot cheaper than the UK where petrol is around £1.55 ($2.64) per litre.

I drove to the airport from Richmond, but from this direction there were no signs for where to drop of car rental returns. I remembered that when I drove through Vancouver from the north, such signs were in place. I drove passed the airport, and managed a U-turn and came back, following the signs for car returns. I finally entered a very large underground car park, and followed the signs for Hertz. An official received the car from me and checked it over. She commented on the large mileage, but it was covered on the unlimited mileage clause thankfully, and it was impossible to penalise me for using the car quite a bit. The rental in total was about £4000, so they've had their money's worth out of me. Provided that the car is rented out continuously, and the evidence is that this is the case, there will easily be enough income from the rental to replace the car every six months if they wanted to, and still have a good profit. They normally replace cars once a year.

I found my way into the terminal which is split into three sections. These are Canada Flights, USA Flights, and International Flights. I didn't know this at first, and the signs were unclear. I realised that my flight was not internal to Canada, so I followed the only other signs from my departure entry. This was to USA Flights, but a large map of the whole world was on each sign, giving rise to the misunderstanding that I was heading for International Flights. You see, this is the problem. The geeks who put all the signs up work here and know the airport like a rabbit knows its warren. I don't. I need clear signage, and I didn't get any. All I got was a straight-talking guy who told me I'd come wrong, and to get back where I'd come from. I had to go back to the area marked Canada Flights, from where there was an offshoot to International Flights.

There was a large queue at the Air Canada desks, but as I had already checked in online, an official told me to proceed directly to security. I had a boarding pass, but only on my phone. I prefer a hardcopy. No need, they said. They happened to be right, but you know the thing. You turn up somewhere with all the evidence you need on the phone, and it won't play because there's no signal, or insufficient battery etc. Anyway, I found security where you and your bag are X-rayed. Then you get reunited with your belongings and toddle off to a flat surface somewhere that you can sort your things out on, and redress yourself.

What always amazes me is the amount of carry-on luggage that people have with them. You are meant to have one small case that will fit in the gauge cage at the check-in desk. Most people bring cases that will not fit in the gauge, and another large bag besides. Then at the gate, they are asking for volunteers to have some of their luggage commuted to the airplane hold. The simple answer is to filter the excess baggage out at the check-in desk, not let them get as far as the plane gate before doing something about it. They give you a maximum size of carry-on bag, and they should stick to it and make all these nuisances either bring less with them, or transfer it to the hold before security. I only have a small case with me that holds everything I need. Plus, I have a very small shoulder bag that holds the sweets supplied by my pharmacy, to keep my bodily parameters in order each day. I also keep my paperwork in the shoulder bag, and my TomTom which is the size of a mobile phone.

I was 7 hours early, so I bought a meal, and watched the lightning flashing, and listening to the roar of thunder, while I filled in my last day's notes. I spent some time looking round the maze of duty-free shops, but as is common, the prices between them are fixed, so that you gain nothing by looking round. Duty-free shopping is a gimmick that many people fall for. As a general rule, the stuff you can buy in a duty-free area, is available more cheaply in the supermarket when you get home. The other advantage of waiting until you arrive is that you don't have to lug the bottles or whatever around the airport with you. Apart from using time and smiling about the prices, I never buy anything here.

Eventually, boarding time came, and as I alluded to earlier, volunteers were asked for to part with some of their luggage for hold storage. I saw nobody go forward, and as a result, when the plane was boarded, items were being stowed under seats because the overhead lockers were full. It really isn't ideal, and care should be taken at the check-in stage to filter large, heavy, and excessive items out.

The plane was late leaving because we had to wait for a connecting flight from Victoria. Then we had to wait for another slot in the queue for take-off because our slot had been lost. However, once we were airborne the pilot announced that he would endeavour to make up the time. Planes don't fly in the lines you would expect. Among the reasons for this is the direction and route of trade winds. If a plane flies in the trade wind, a faster speed with less fuel use is achieved. We flew what is called the polar route, travelling north and then over Greenland before crossing Iceland and down through England to Heathrow. The flight is nearly 5000 miles, and the plane achieved this in 8.5 hours. Passing over Greenland, the northern lights were clearly visible with curtains of green across the sky. I couldn't get a good photo because I had by choice an aisle seat, but the view was nice. The flight was uneventful and, though there was some turbulence, as usual, it was mostly mild. The plane landed in London Heathrow at 1pm. Passing through Heathrow was a dream. I had no hold luggage, and was therefore on my way to passport control while the general melee was waiting for their bags to come round the carousel. Passport control was simple. I had to place my passport in a scanner while having my face photographed. The two images didn't match, so I had to try again, keeping a stern face, and looking the lens in the eye. The second time, the match must have been made because the two leaved doors opened and I was on my way. I asked directions to the Underground, and the official happened to be going off duty, and he took me. Basically, you go out of the front door of Terminal 2, which is called the "Queen's Terminal", and make for lifts, which descend to the Underground level, and then you walk down a couple of corridors to the Underground station. It could all be signed better, but it isn't. The reason is that the signage is done by people who know the area intimately. They'd do better by asking a stranger like me to tell them where to put the signs. It's quite simple really, but so are the people doing the signage. The Underground is a frequently used method of getting from Heathrow to Central London. All you need is a ruck of Underground Train signs in big lettering, and start placing them immediately after passport control, and repeat them at every direction change until you come to the platform.

Once I reached the Underground, I presented my paid for ticket, and the barrier would not open. That normally happens. If there is an official handy, you show your ticket and they use a pass to open the barrier. If there is no official, you follow another person through the barrier. You aren't supposed to do that, but if you've paid for the ticket and the technology is being obtuse, I think the follow through method is acceptable. I only had to wait 1 minute for the next train, and whatever people tell you, it's best to stay on it until you get to Green Park. Here, you swap to the Victoria Line and get off at Euston. My train was meant to leave Euston for Birmingham New Street at 15:36. I was actually in time to catch the earlier train. They run about once per hour. However, you are only allowed to travel on the service for which your ticket time matches. Having an hour to kill, I made my way to the third floor at Euston Station, where there is a lovely pub, and I medically benefitted from a pint of London Pride. How good it was to have a real live ale after nearly six weeks of suds, apart from a few exceptions!

My train left on time at 15:36 and made its way up through England to Birmingham. Passing Oxford, I had a message from work, asking for me to support the late shift tomorrow. There's nothing like getting back to it at once. I also had a message from Andy, a friend at Selattyn, asking to give me a lift home from Gobowen Station. At Birmingham I had to wait about 20 minutes for the through train to Gobowen, but that too, left on time, and I rolled into Gobowen at 18:43. Andy and his wife Ali met me and we had some more medication at The Royal Oak before finally reaching home at 20:30.

Conclusion

Thus ends my epic trip across Canada, full of sights and sounds of this wonderful country. There have been highs and lows, such as happen on all trips. The overriding feeling is one of the magnificent scenery and interesting wildlife. I have not seen all I would like to have done, but feel very blessed with such as I have been able to enjoy.

My total journey length in the hire car was 12870 km (8000 miles) in a route roughly shown below.

Had more time and funds been available, I would like to have visited Churchill by using the railway, and see the polar bears in their natural habitat. I'd like to have explored some of the northern territories and the Yukon, and see grizzly bears. I'd like to have seen more black bears up close. News is just in of a black bear who got into a shop in Vancouver Island and helped himself to a packet of bear gummies, and fled. I'd love an encounter like that. I'd also like to see not one moose, but a herd of them, and the same goes for caribou.

Maybe time will present another opportunity to fulfil these wishes, but for now, I have lots of memories that I have enjoyed sharing with you.

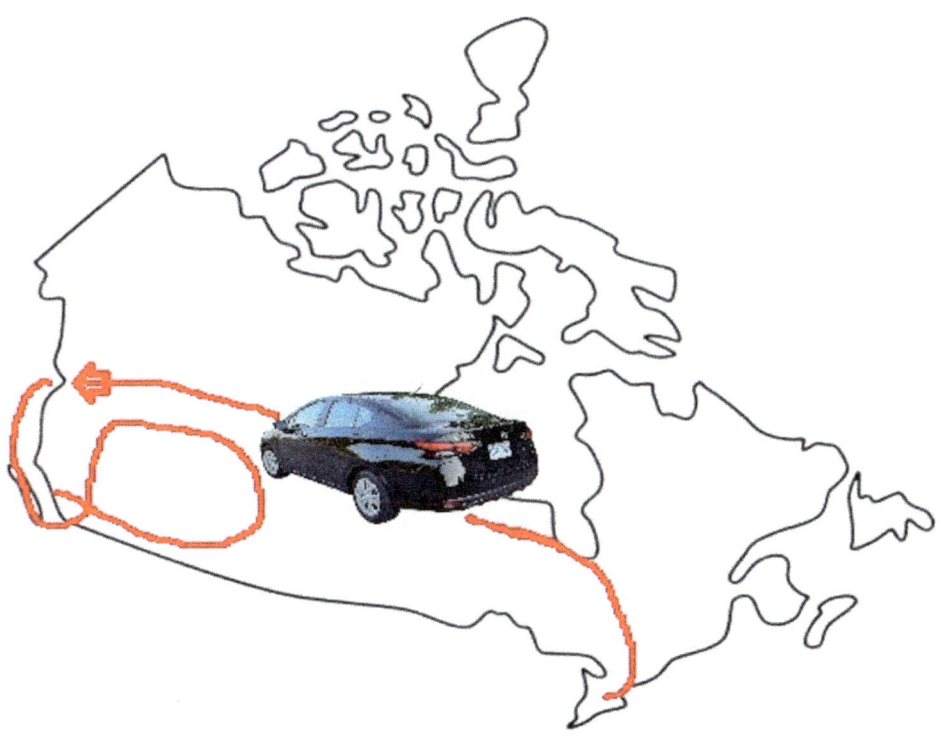

www.ingramcontent.com/pod-product-compliance
Lightning Source LLC
Chambersburg PA
CBHW061208230426
43665CB00028B/2954